TEACH YOURSELF FORTUNE TELLING

TEACH YOURSELF

FORTUNE TELLING

Palmistry, The Crystal Ball, Runes, Tea Leaves, The Tarot

RACHEL POLLACK

An Owl Book
HENRY HOLT AND COMPANY
NEW YORK

To Ronnie Dreyer

Published in the United States by Henry Holt and Company, Inc.,
521 Fifth Avenue, New York, New York 10175.
Originally published in Great Britain under the title
A Practical Guide to Fortune Telling.

Library of Congress Cataloging-in-Publication Data

Pollack, Rachel.
Teach yourself fortune telling.

"An Owl book."
1. Fortune-telling. 2. Divination. I. Title.
BF1861.P65 1986 133.3'24 86-7664

ISBN 0-8050-0125-5 (pbk.)

First American Edition

This book was designed and produced by
The Rainbird Publishing Group Limited
27 Wrights Lane
London W8 5TZ

Printed in Great Britain

1 3 5 7 9 10 8 6 4 2

ISBN 0-8050-0125-5

Facing page: Consulting the astrologer, from a seventeenth-century woodcut. Many methods of fortune telling have evolved down the centuries in attempts to read the character and destiny of individuals.

CONTENTS

LIST OF DRAWINGS

INTRODUCTION

In ancient China, 3,400 years ago, if a king wished to know whether or not to launch a military campaign or hunting expedition, or to find out whether the following days would bring good fortune, he would call in a large group of priests, interpreters and other officials. These advisers would take the shell of a turtle and heat it until cracks appeared on the surface. By the shape of the cracks they would tell the king the shape of the future. The practice continued for at least 1,500 years. The following invocation dates from about 100 BC: 'Commit unto us, thy eternal truth, O mighty turtle, that we, by thy power, might be guided in our choice. . . .'

Today, people all over the world seek guidance in their lives by tossing three coins six times until, by the way the coins fall, they discover a 'hexagram' of six lines. They then look up that particular hexagram (one of sixty-four possible) in what many consider the world's oldest book – the *I Ching*, or *Book of Changes*, composed in China some time during the age of the burnt turtle shells.

Ancient methods of divination varied according to region. In the Middle East dead animals were cut up and the shape and colour of their entrails examined. Among the Hittites the practice became so complex that one engraving cites the inspection of the innards of thirty-four sheep and twenty birds. In Babylon the official soothsayers used to drop flour into a dish of water. The lumps into which the flour congealed were believed to form definite patterns. Here is a sample reading of one of these:

> If the flour, in the east, takes the shape of a lion's face, the man is in the grip of a ghost of one who lies in the open country: the sun will consign it [the ghost] to the wind and he will get well.

Consulting the 'sticks of fate' to foretell events by the I Ching. *This ancient Chinese text, at least 4,000 years old, is both a philosophical system and a method of divination greatly revered in the East and now widely used in the West. Many ordinary people consult the oracle for advice on their problems.*

Today, in most large American cities, countless shop windows display the words 'Reader-Adviser', along with a selection of Tarot cards, a crystal ball, a diagram of a hand and sometimes a plastic model of a human head.

The desire to forecast future events is one of the great constants of human history. People have used virtually every aspect of existence as aids to fortune telling or divination, to give it its proper name. Everyone has heard of astrology, in which we seek to understand human life by studying the grand movements of the planets through the twelve star constellations of the zodiac. But what of tyromancy – divination by studying cheese? Or stolisomancy – finding omens in the peculiarities of people's dress?

The term 'divination' implies the belief that fortune telling, or seeking omens, was a way of allowing the divine voice to speak to us. Nowadays few people believe that this is so. Yet they still wonder why and how fortune telling works. Or does it work? It is hard to answer this question without reference to personal experience. Almost anyone who has consulted the *I Ching* for any length of time will vouch for its astounding precision in describing people's lives. The same holds true for the Tarot. Recently I did a joint reading for two people. Eight of the twelve cards had also appeared in their most recent readings. Moreover, those eight were the ones they had each previously singled out as the most vital images. They had written about them in their journals and used them in meditations. The other four cards also described their situation with great accuracy. Perhaps most interesting, all of us were so used to this kind of connection with the Tarot that none of us took notice of the 'coincidence' until after the reading.

If we accept that divination does produce meaningful results, we still cannot say exactly what happens. The question is highly complex but we can attempt a brief answer. Let us suppose that the seemingly random events of life actually form patterns. These patterns shift and re-form continually but they are always there, under the surface, at a level we might call the 'world of patterns'. Normal perception does not allow us to see these

The sacrifice of animals to enable divination by the appearance of their entrails (or haruspicy), was widely practised by the ancient Romans, as seen in this marble relief. The Romans established a special priesthood for this purpose, whose members were known as 'augurs'. Augurs were appointed for life and their office was one of great power and dignity. They were responsible for interpreting the will of the gods and foretelling future events.

shapes in our lives since we do not know how to look beyond our immediate experience. We can, however, approach the underlying patterns indirectly. For this hidden world bears a peculiar feature. Any one pattern connects with all the other kinds of patterns and any method that allows bits and pieces to come together without conscious control can be used. These can include mixing cards, watching the way a flame rises from an oil lamp, swirling tea leaves round a cup, or even watching the eating patterns of sacred chickens.

Most methods of divination fall into one of two categories. The first involves a fixed system of information. Let us use the Tarot as an example. The deck contains seventy-eight cards, each with its own meaning, such as 'journey by water' or 'success through willpower'. The subject of the reading mixes the cards and the reader lays them out in a definite pattern. Each position in this pattern also carries a meaning, such as 'coming events' or 'influence of others'. The reading consists of the overall message formed by the cards and their placings.

The second method produces an actual image, which can be called a 'sign' or an 'omen'. Physical objects are thrown together until a picture emerges. For instance, we might toss pebbles on to the ground to see if any recognizable images form by the way they fall. Tea leaf reading belongs to this method. The leaves form clumps and the reader checks to see if these clumps resemble acorns, birds, horses, or other familiar pictures.

With both methods, interpretation requires a mixture of knowledge and sensitivity. With the Tarot you need, first and foremost, to know the meanings of the cards but you also have to develop a feeling for the way they come together. The card of Strength will have a different meaning beside the Knight of Swords than it will beside the Ace of Wands. Many of the cards will carry several possible meanings. With practice the reader can sense which of these is most applicable to the situation.

Something similar occurs in such divination methods as tea leaf reading or crystal ball gazing. An image forms. We might assume that having a picture makes it easy to interpret. Sometimes this will be the case. You might see the face of someone you know and you can guess that this person will influence your life in some way. Even here, however, you still need to determine the kind of influence that the person will have on you. And very few of the images will ever appear so obvious. Mostly, they will form symbols. You look in your teacup and see an outline of a lion. But what does that mean?

In fact there are long lists of meanings for such techniques as tea leaf reading and the chapter on tea leaves includes the more common symbols and their traditional interpretations. The reader who simply checks the list will, however, miss a vital part of divination. For if you look at the images – the lion, or the boat, or the book – if you open yourself to it, allow it to stir your imagination and connect with the question and the subject of the reading, you will discover that your interpretation becomes more accurate and more beneficial, for it will go more deeply into the truth of the situation.

A reading of any kind should form a worthwhile (some say 'healing') experience. There is no point in telling someone's fortune if it scares the person or prevents him or her from making decisions and acting upon them. Unpleasant readings do occur, of course, just as unpleasant things happen in life. If the reading appears to show something painful or difficult, first think again about your interpretation. Perhaps you have exaggerated the importance of some particular sign. Many people are naturally pessimistic. If they see one disturbing sign or omen in a reading filled with wonderful things, they will focus on this to the exclusion of everything else.

If you feel certain about the meaning, consider it next as a possible warning. Does the reading suggest steps to take that will alter the unpleasant result? Perhaps the person can avoid doing something by, for example, staying at home or going somewhere else if the reading clearly describes a planned weekend trip as a disaster. Or maybe the subject can take a more cautious approach to a situation by not, for example, rushing into a love affair but getting to know the other person better before making a commitment.

Remember that the signs and omens do not control our actions. They do not even tell the future. What they show is the current pattern, the way things are heading now under the prevailing influences. While these influences may affect us very powerfully they do not take away our freedom to direct our own lives. However, the reading can help us use that freedom to direct our lives in a beneficial way.

Curiously, we also need to treat joyful readings with care. For just as few readings predict inevitable difficulties, so few readings show inevitable happiness. Often, if the signs point to a beneficial development, they really say, 'This *can* happen providing the person takes the right approach.' The reader should then point out what the subject needs to do to help the outcome emerge.

Some of these ideas may appear slightly unusual. After all, don't fortune tellers predict the future? In recent years divination has undergone a strong revival. At the same time a more modern approach has evolved. Diviners now seek to understand the moment, rather than tell the future. This moment, however, reaches both backwards – showing what happened in the past to produce the present situation – and forward – revealing the likely results if they continue in the same direction. Very often the reading *will* show future events and influences. Such things as new love affairs, travel, the influence of others – all these and more will show up in a reading. The pattern extends into the future in ways that our conscious minds cannot recognize.

If all this sounds complicated, it is. Not every reading will show such complex issues. If you are just beginning with divination, you will probably find many of your readings simple – or confusing. The subtleties, however, remain under the surface (this holds especially for the more complex systems such as Tarot or Runes). As you become more experienced you will find yourself discovering combinations and influences that you would have missed when you first began.

Just as modern divination focuses on influences rather than events, so it also tends to emphasize psychology and character analysis. We will see that this applies especially to palmistry. For instance, modern palmists no longer consider the heart line as a predictor of marriage and children. Instead, they look at what the heart line says about how the person will behave when married. Something of the same approach applies to any of the methods described in this book. If modern diviners returned to heating turtle shells, they would probably interpret the cracks in terms of the person's character, and influences on his or her life.

Most people assume that we tell fortunes in order to discover secrets. While it is certainly true that information remains the primary purpose of divination, the practice actually leads to other benefits as well. Divination opens you to an awareness of patterns in life. Through readings, and thinking about them and trying to explain, you begin to notice how different people and events influence each other and how things come together in ways that the conscious mind might not have noticed. You will see, for example, how a certain period in someone's life may bring happiness, while another person in the same position may experience a string of problems. In short, divination increases your perceptions about people and in order to understand your readings better, you will need to become a student of human nature.

Divination can also develop your sensitivity to others. You may need tact in explaining the meanings. You will need to know when not to say things. If you think your comments might frighten someone or over-influence their actions and choices, you had best keep silent.

Divination will develop your intuition. Several interpretations may be possible for a single aspect of the reading and with experience you will find that one (or more than one) feels right. You cannot give a logical reason for this, you simply know. Divination works as a kind of exercise programme for intuition, insight and rational analysis.

You will find insight and analysis especially important in the more fixed systems. Tarot, the Runes, and palmistry will increase your perceptions as well as your ability to think in complex terms. This happens because they provide so much information that you need to learn how to synthesize it all.

The other kind of divination, with its created images, depends more on intuition and the ability to feel the inner truth of a symbol. The pictures on a Tarot card are symbolic but the symbols are the same for everyone. Particular tea leaf patterns, however, did not exist before the person swirled the leaves about, and they will vanish for ever as soon as the cup is washed. With the crystal ball, the images do not even exist in a physical form. The mind calls them up directly from the unconscious.

Whichever methods of divination you choose, certain general points will apply. Be careful of becoming dependent on fortune telling. Many people, especially when they first start, check their cards or tea leaves before making any decision, no matter how small. Until you understand the limits of divination and what a reading can and cannot tell you, take all your readings with a measure of scepticism.

This does not mean that divination should be treated as a joke or a game. You will get the best results when you approach a reading with a sincere desire to see what the oracle can tell you about your question. If people at a party ask you to tell their fortunes, think twice before agreeing. For one thing, you might find that the person's frivolous attitude makes it difficult for you to focus on the signs. On the other hand, the reading might penetrate more deeply than the subject expected. I once read the Tarot cards for an acquaintance who claimed that he was curious but didn't believe in 'that kind of thing'. We ended up by spending an hour and a half discussing various problems in his marriage. I had known nothing about these before turning over the cards to begin the reading.

Before you begin a reading take a few moments to 'centre' yourself. This involves calming the body and mind. Sit straight and close your eyes. Breathe deeply but naturally, taking the breath all the way down to the diaphragm and releasing it gently. Allow your body to relax and, as you feel the tension slide away, try to let go of extraneous thoughts and worries, including the question you wish to ask. Simply try to clear your mind and to focus on the cards, crystal ball, stones or whatever system you are about to use. If you can, feel a line or some other connection joining you to the oracle. Continue to breathe easily and deeply, and as you do so, feel that you are going inside yourself to a place where you can know and see what normally remains hidden. When you feel yourself connected and totally relaxed, open your eyes and begin the reading.

Centring is a simple form of meditation. It not only awakens the intuition but also helps you consider any difficult parts of the reading without getting upset. As with any form of meditation, to begin with you will probably feel that it just doesn't work. You might even find yourself more rather than less tense. But it is worth continuing for eventually you will discover that these few minutes before the reading greatly increase your ability to sense the truth concealed within the omens. In a certain sense the centring may become more important than the reading itself.

PALMISTRY

INTRODUCTION

Palmistry traditionally belongs to the world of fortune telling. The shop window displaying a crystal ball and the drawing of a mysterious woman with piercing eyes will always include a diagram of a hand along with two or three Tarot cards. And yet, palmistry is, in many ways, the opposite of divination. For if divination means reaching into the unknown 'world of patterns', in palmistry the pattern lies right in front of us, in our own hands. While divination works by throwing together random pieces of information, there is nothing random about palmistry. The lines, the mounts, the finger shapes are all there, ready for interpretation. Finally, where a Tarot reading, a look into a crystal or a casting of the Runes will show the *moment* – what is happening now with a projection into the future – palmistry shows a life. Like astrology, palmistry is concerned with the whole person.

Since it gives an overall view, palmistry is more complicated than most other methods of fortune telling. Whereas a Tarot reading can answer a specific question, blocking out the other features of a person's life and past, the hand shows everything. Certainly you can read the individual lines and shapes separately – there is really no other way to do it – but obtaining a complete picture of what the hand tells you will depend on linking the different pieces of information. For instance, a red palm will sometimes indicate an aggressive personality. But how does this aggression manifest itself? The lines, together with the shapes and developments of the fingers, can indicate such qualities as leadership, sexuality, career potential, artistic talent and so on.

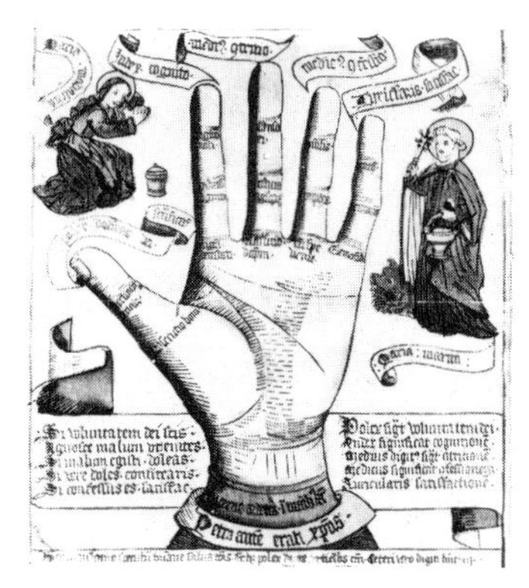

Palmistry, or chiromancy, is another historic and very popular method of attempting to read a person's character. Since ancient times, especially in China and Greece, the lines and ridges of the palm of the hand have served as signs. Many authoritative charts, such as this German engraving of 1466, offered schemes of interpretations.

Any of these can modify that basic aggressive tendency.

Various methods of divination will often predict events. The 5 of Cups in the Tarot will show a loss, the 6 of Pentacles may indicate a gift or the offer of help. Palmistry, however, reveals character traits. It shows the possibilities in life. You may find this idea a little strange. Doesn't your life line tell you when you will die? Don't palmists tell you how many children you will have and what sex they will be? The simple answer, according to many palmists, is no. A short life line does not mean a short life. It may suggest low vitality and the need to conserve energy, or may even mean that the person's ancestors died young, but it does not predict an early death. Similarly, the heart line indicates the way someone experiences emotion rather than specific events such as marriage or divorce. If a palmist says, for example, 'You and your husband will split up in three years', banish such thoughts from your mind. This 'prediction' by the way, is an actual example. Twelve years later the couple were still together.

People think of palmistry as reading the lines in the hand (see Figure 1). In fact, every part of the hand can tell us something. Its very shape and length, the lengths and shapes of the fingers, the texture and colour of the skin, the raised areas (called mounts), all contribute to an understanding. Not only does each finger have a meaning but its three sections, (called phalanges) each have a meaning too.

With rare exceptions, most people favour one hand over the other. Some psychologists believe that right- or left-handedness indicates a development of one side of the brain over the other. Since each half of the brain governs particular qualities, left-handed people supposedly behave differently to right-handed people. Such ideas might seem to reawaken old prejudices against left-handedness (in the past teachers sometimes tied the left hand behind the back to force left-handed children to use the right). Palmistry takes another approach. Although the distinction between one hand and the other matters a great deal, whether the right or left dominates is immaterial. Let us call the favoured hand 'major' and the other hand 'minor'. For right-handed people, the right is the major and the left the minor. For those who are left-handed, the reverse is true. The difference is this: the major hand shows

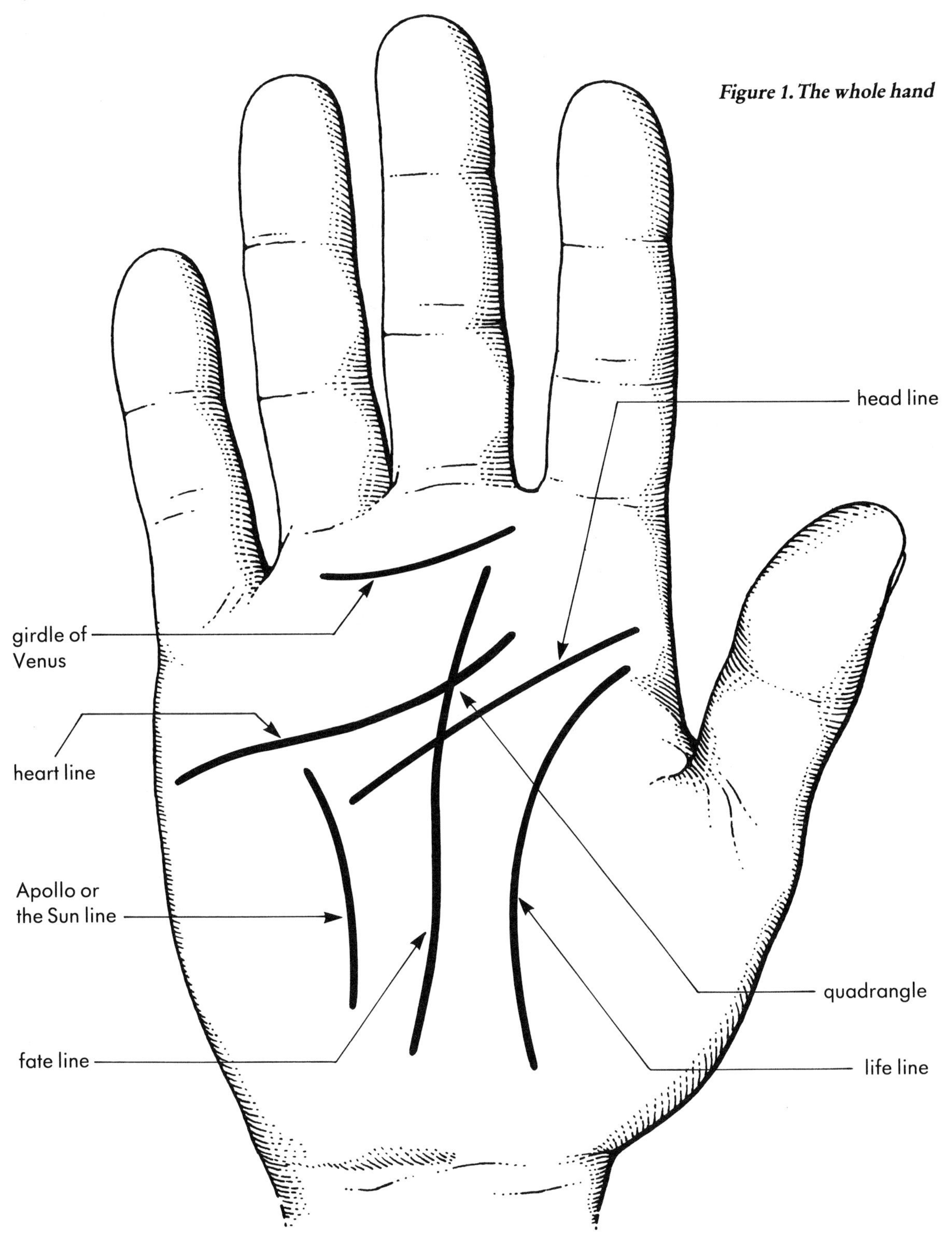

Figure 1. The whole hand

what a person has made of his or her life – who he or she is now; the minor reveals the subject's history – who the person was when younger and where he or she has come from.

We all make our own history. Life gives us certain possibilities and directions, uniqe for each of us, which we can develop in any number of ways. The minor hand, then, indicates the 'given' potential in life, while the major shows how this has been used. An example makes the distinction clear. The subject was a right-handed woman. The right hand, the major, showed no fate line. This does not indicate anything ominous (see below) but it does describe a person who has made their own way in the world rather than simply following the pattern determined by parents or society. The left hand, however, the minor, did show a fate line, although one relatively weaker than the other lines of the hand. I interpreted this faintness of line to mean that, when young, the woman conformed to people's expectations, although only in her outward behaviour. The fate line appeared in her minor hand but not in her major because she had not created her own path until later in life. Similarly, the left hand showed more complex lines although the lines in the right hand were deeper. Once the woman followed her own choices, her life became simpler and stronger.

The example of the missing line raises an important point. Virtually every hand will show the three major lines: fate, head, and heart, just as every hand will have some of the mounts, certainly the mount of Venus at the bottom of the thumb. No hand, however, will exhibit all of the lines described in palmistry and no hand will display every mount prominently. A missing line or a flat mount does not, therefore, indicate impending disaster or weakness and should not be given too much importance. The hand will undoubtedly show enough other features to put the missing point in a wider perspective.

The interpretations given here (and in any book on palmistry) are guidelines only. Reality will always modify them. Always talk over the meanings with your subject and explore together the ways in which the hand shows how his or her life has developed. One important point: make sure that what you interpret comes from the actual qualities of the hand and not from external factors. In considering the texture and colour of the hand (such as the aggressive red palm mentioned earlier), you should find out the person's occupation. Are they a dishwasher, a stevedore, a typist, or a model? Do they use hand creams? Try to detect innate softness or roughness beneath the outer conditions. Diseases can play a part as well. While enlarged knuckles can indicate a need for order and routine, they can also result from arthritis or injury.

All methods of interpreting the world bring out its contradictions. Philosophers will argue with great passion the relative truths of pragmatism, idealism, and materialism just as psychologists divide themselves into groups such as Freudians, behaviourists, and humanists. So do not expect uniformity among palmists. They will agree as to the lines and markings they are studying since tradition indicates general ways of looking at these things. When it gets down to details, however, each palmist will work from their own system. This book will show you how to begin. Other books will provide more detailed refinements of technique – and more contradictions. Do not

'The prophet of St Paul's', an engraving by Charles Heath after a painting by A. E. Heath. By the seventeenth century in Europe palmistry was at the height of its popularity and textbooks on the subject flooded the market.

hesitate to question interpretations. Compare what you see in the hand (and read from books) as much as possible with what you know of the reality. This is especially important when starting out, for when we know little, we tend to accept totally the pronouncements of authority. Use this book to guide you but keep an open mind. Eventually you will develop your own methods and system.

COLOUR, TEXTURE, AND SHAPE

Begin by looking at the hand as a whole. Does the skin feel coarse or fine? (Remember to account for the kind of work the person does and such treatments as hand creams.) Is its natural colour pale, pink, or red? (Although these tones refer primarily to white people, the concept of dark and light shades in the palm is universal.) Is the hand large or small, thick or thin?

Very smooth skin suggests sensitivity and an aesthetic awareness, possibly artistic skill. Naturally coarse skin (not from chapping or manual work) indicates someone with a strong constitution, as well as someone not overly bothered by the opinions of others. Thin hands are versatile; thick hands are dextrous but denote stubbornness. Hands that are thin, soft, and narrow may indicate weakness or indecision but also quick reactions.

We can usually say that the darker the colour of the skin, the more outgoing and aggressive the subject. Pale hands indicate introspection. Pink hands show someone outgoing but sympathetic to others. Bright red palms can signify an aggressive tendency. A bright pink colour may point to high blood pressure (just as a yellowish, dry palm may indicate kidney trouble). However, this or any medical diagnosis made through palmistry (or divination of any sort) should always be checked by a medical examination.

The size of the hand often bears an inverse relationship to ambition. Small hands look for big projects. Large hands, however, are said to work easily with small objects.

From size, texture, and colour we move on to the shape of the palm. Ask the subject to hold out both hands in front of you. Do the sides of the palm appear straight or curved? Is the palm wider at the top than the bottom? Are the sides longer than the distance across the fingers? Palmists have observed three major types of hand and two less common sorts. We will look at the three basic varieties first.

COMMON HAND TYPES

Square (see Figure 2): Square-palmed people, especially those with square-shaped fingers, are hard-working and productive. They value results more than large plans but, with other indications such as ambition and imagination, make good managers. Some palmists consider them conventional and conformist, while others emphasize their ability to adapt and make the most of what life has given them. Large, square hands denote great strength, while small, square hands show perseverance. A square palm with long fingers will signify high achievement – ambition mixed with productivity.

Conic, Round, or Oval (see Figure 3): Many people consider this sort of hand 'feminine' or 'pretty'. It is marked by a round palm, usually smooth skin, often with tapered fingers. This hand indicates imagination but without the square-shaped sense of structure or the spatulate hand's need for novelty and adventure. Many people think of conic hands as indicating an artist but they can also signify laziness and a love of luxury. These people are sociable, warm, and trusting, with a strong nesting instinct. Sometimes they can fall too easily under the influence of others. A flexible conic hand, with smooth skin, a well-developed middle finger, and a cross or a star in the centre of the palm traditionally signifies great psychic ability.

Spatulate (see Figure 4): In this type of hand the palm is usually wider across the fingers than at the base, although the opposite is also found. In general, the spatulate hand indicates people who love the new and unconventional. They may gravitate to unusual friends. At the same time, spatulate hands often signify a willingness to work hard. These people expect great effort from others as well as themselves. If broader at the base, the spatulate hand reveals a need for physical activity. If broader at the top, the desire for novelty translates to mental stimulation, a love of ideas but also the armchair explorer who is happy to stay at home and share the adventures of others vicariously.

Common types of hand

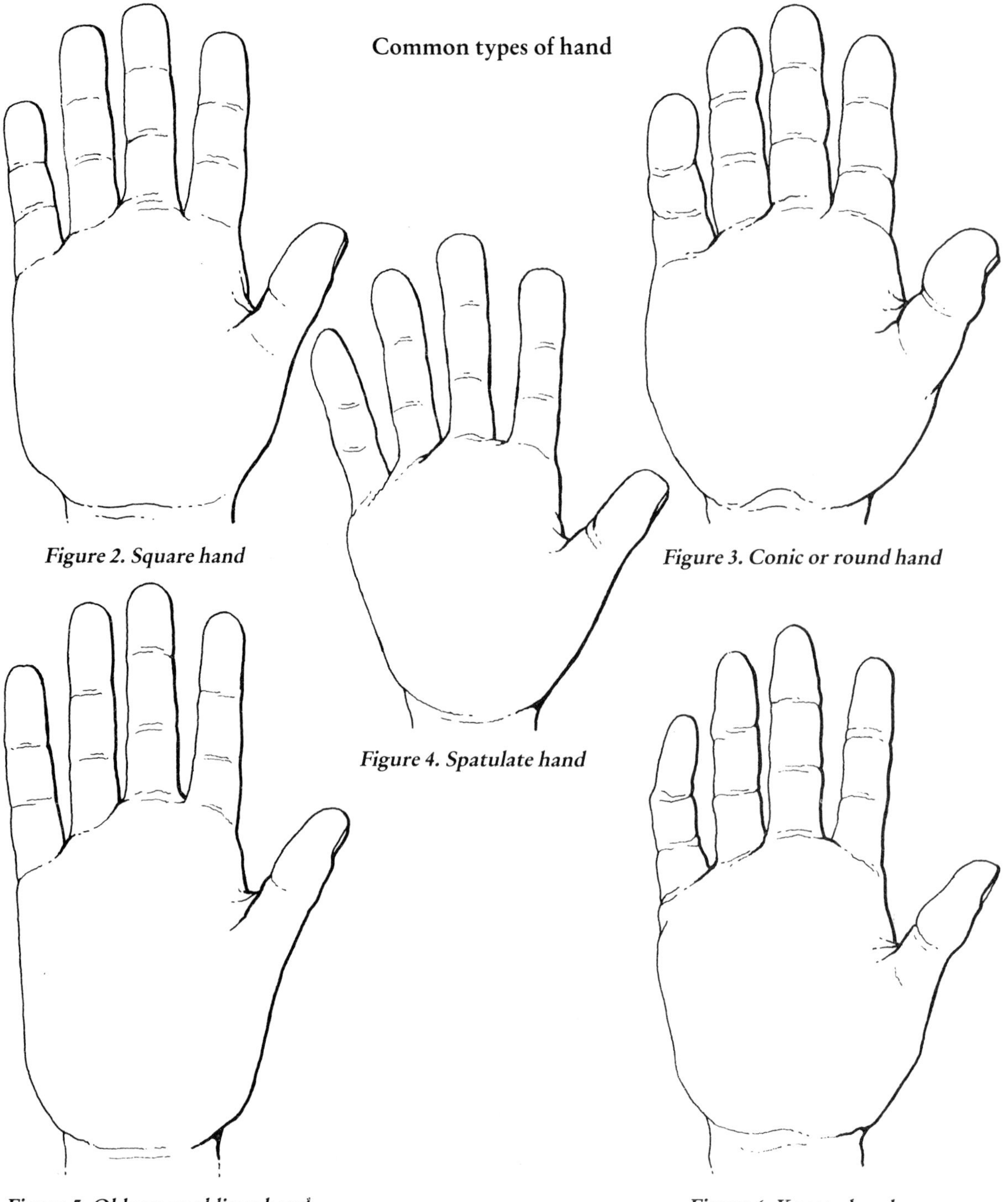

Figure 2. Square hand

Figure 3. Conic or round hand

Figure 4. Spatulate hand

Figure 5. Oblong or oblique hand

Figure 6. Knotty hand

LESS COMMON HAND TYPES

Oblong or Oblique (see Figure 5)*:* This type resembles the square hand with its straight sides and its equal width at top and bottom. It differs from the square palm in being noticeably longer than wide. Traditionally, palmists have seen this hand as signifying weakness, fear of responsibility, and submission to dominant parents or partners. However, a more modern view regards this hand as indicating sensitivity and careful thought. The person may appear shy but this comes from a deliberate working out of experience. People with oblong palms may have to work harder to realize their potential but that potential may be very strong.

Knotty (see Figure 6)*:* This sort of hand may look unattractive owing to the pronounced joints of the fingers and the concave sides of the palms. It indicates great imagination and originality, however, with a high level of concentration. This subject can become very absorbed in creative work, especially of an academic or scientific nature, but may lack a sense of humour or an awareness of life's practical obligations.

These palm shapes are ideals and you may find it hard to identify a hand as being one sort or another. You may also discover mixtures, such as a square hand with spatulate fingers or a conic hand with some fingers conic but others square or pointed. Try to understand the shapes and how they combine.

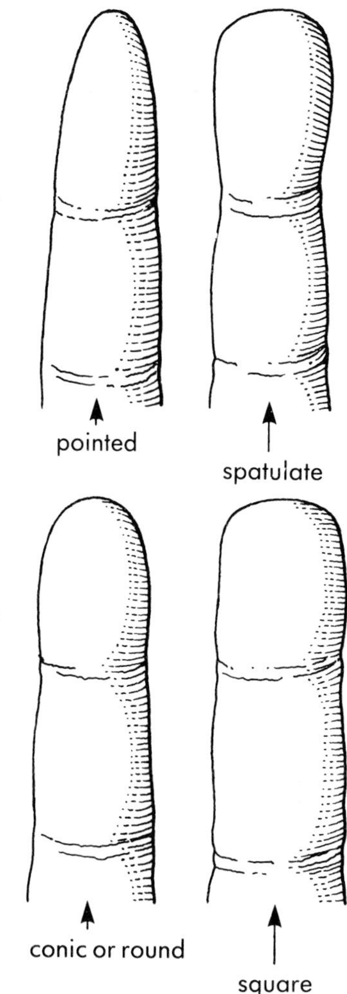

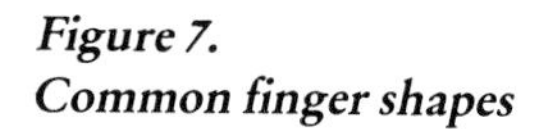

Figure 7.
Common finger shapes

FINGER SHAPES

The fingertips have similar shapes to the palms and, in fact, the 'true' hand shape will show the same sort of palm as fingers (see Figure 7). In other words, square palms and square fingers together make up the square hand. In practice we not only find some hands where the fingers contrast with the palm but also some where they differ from each other. Since each finger carries its own meanings, each can be looked at individually and we can say, for instance, that the index finger (denoting leadership and the way one relates to others), shows a square approach, while the ring finger (denoting art and creativity) takes a spiritual approach.

Square: These fingertips indicate an analytical approach, a love of detail in one's own work and the work of others.

Pointed: These fingertips, sometimes called 'psychic', show a quick mind which absorbs impressions and ideas with ease. They indicate the person's desire to communicate and express themselves and someone with sharp perceptions.

Round: These fingertips signify a love of beauty or harmony. Their owners need tranquillity but care deeply about others.

Spatulate: These fingertips show a need for activity, movement, and excitement. Their owners take an original approach to problems and ideas and are often unconventional. If the fingertips flare out from a point at the base of the nail (rather than the more common, rounded base) they may indicate someone who, from enthusiasm, takes on too many responsibilities, spreading his or her energy too thinly.

THE FINGERS

The fingers bear names from classical mythology (see Figure 8). Actually the names derive from the planets, with the Apollo finger also called the Sun finger (Apollo was the Greek god of the sun). These traditional designations link palmistry to astrology and, in fact, the meanings of the fingers resemble the astrological influences of the particular planets. Palmistry carries its own tradition, however, and you do not need to be familiar with astrology to understand the fingers.

Before looking at the individual fingers, we need to consider overall lengths. We mark these according to the longest finger which is the middle or Saturn finger. Measure it with a ruler, then measure the length of the palm. Seven-eighths of the palm is considered average. More than seven-eighths we call long, less we call short.

People with long fingers tend to take a mental approach to life. They are contemplative but can also immerse themselves in detail or digressions. They show a sense of idealism and loyalty.

Short fingers indicate a physical nature, someone who likes activity, movement, and exercise. Short-fingered people are enthusiastic, both about new projects and about friends. At the same time they may lack the patience to follow things through. Since they prefer to look at life in a direct way, friends may find them blunt.

In considering the phalanges as a group, we again look at which phalanx (if any) dominates the others. Traditionally, palmists assign the following proportions to the phalanges: two to the first (nearest the fingertip), two and a half to the second, three to the third. The actual lengths do not matter as much as the comparison of one with the other. If one set of phalanges, the first, the second, or the third, appears noticeably longer than the average in all the fingers, this suggests that the person has developed that area more fully than the others. For instance, if the first phalanges are longer, and especially if they also appear full and wide, then he or she shows a strong spiritual instinct. If the second phalanges dominate, the subject will take a mental

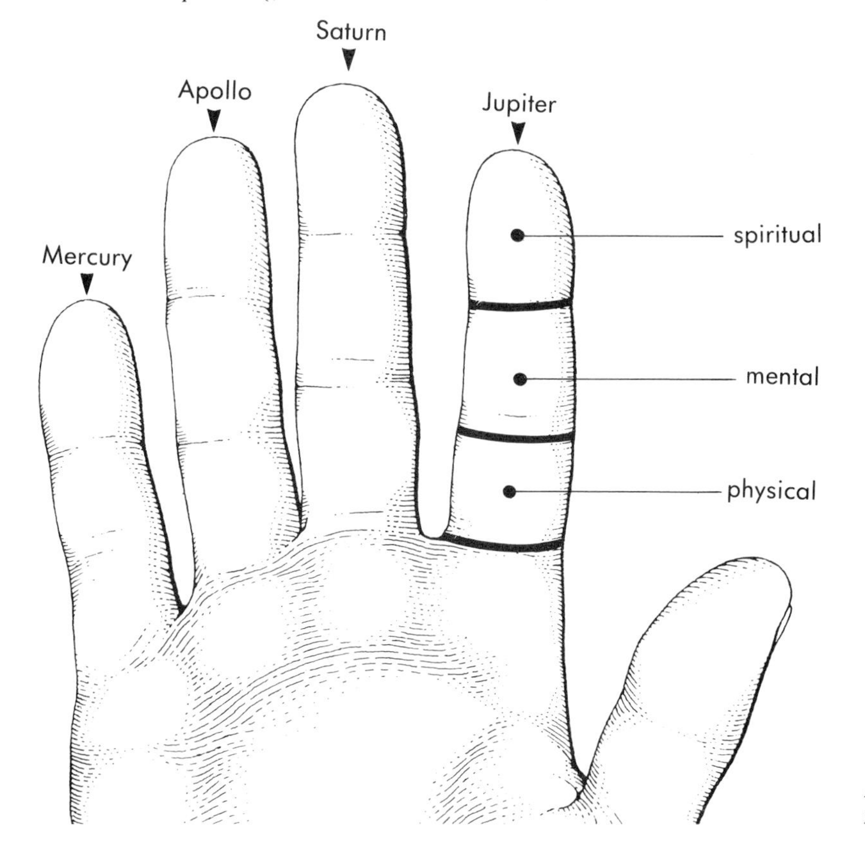

Figure 8. Names of the fingers and phalanges

approach to the world, analysing life and experience and loving ideas. Long but narrow middle phalanges may indicate strongly held but narrow beliefs. Similarly, puffy middle phalanges may signify smugness and conceit about mental abilities.

The third phalanx, closest to the palm, describes the physical approach to life. These phalanges are usually the longest, showing how our physical needs determine so much of our lives. If even longer than usual, they denote a tendency to take life in a very physical way, without analysis or much spiritual consideration. The fuller the third phalanges, the more the subject seeks comfort and sensual indulgence.

So far, we have looked at finger lengths and phalanges as a whole. As we move to the individual fingers, we again consider lengths. Here too we measure them against each other, calling a finger long if it reaches beyond the average proportions. Each finger relates to a specific part of life. If a particular finger appears long in relation to the others, we can guess that the person shows a strong interest or development in that area. Furthermore, if a certain phalanx is more prominent, this will tell us something about the way a subject expresses him or herself in the area that the finger represents. This sounds more complicated than it is. Consider an example. The index (or Jupiter) finger indicates an individual's relations with the outside world and particularly with other people. If this finger appears long in proportion to the middle finger, we can expect the person to show leadership qualities. But what sort of leadership? The phalanges can give a clue. If the first phalanx is longer and/or wider than usual, he or she will lead in some spiritual way, perhaps literally, as a minister, or more personally, by inspiring others. If the second phalanx is stronger, then the leadership comes out in a mental way, through ideas or a strong personality. A dominant last phalanx would indicate physical leadership, either in sports, or simply in a powerful physical presence. As a further refinement, if the important phalanx appears puffy as well as wide and long, this may suggest an abuse of that leadership potential just as puffiness can signify self-indulgence.

The Jupiter Finger: The Jupiter finger represents relationships with others, particularly in terms of authority and leadership. It can also indicate protective feelings, someone with a strong maternal or paternal instinct. The talent of a natural teacher may show in a strong Jupiter finger. Its connection with the outside world means that the Jupiter finger represents curiosity and a desire to explore.

The Jupiter finger is of average length if it reaches halfway up the top phalanx of the middle finger. The average Jupiter finger also matches the length of the Apollo or ring finger. It will signify a person who gets along with others and who is not easily led but not overly dominant either. A longer than normal Jupiter finger shows a strong leadership capacity, while a short one may represent someone who feels a lack of confidence about facing the world and needs to follow others. A short Jupiter finger can denote a weak ego and someone lacking in confidence. However, it can also suggest tact and consideration. If the finger appears strong and firm, then the shortness may not indicate serious problems.

As well as the length and thickness of a finger, palmists also look at any bends or leanings. With the Jupiter finger such variations indicate that the person sees the world differently from others. If the first phalanx bends towards the Saturn finger, however, this may increase the suggestion of leadership.

The Saturn Finger: Since we tend to judge the other fingers by the Saturn, we may find it difficult to see it as long or short. But if all the others are in proportion to each other and Saturn stands out in some way, an assessment can be made.

In astrology Saturn symbolizes limitations and problems but also the lessons we learn from them. The Saturn finger has some of the same characteristics, particularly regarding the way we face problems and responsibilities. It also indicates a balanced approach to life. An average Saturn finger, therefore, denotes equanimity and the ability to deal with the world.

A long Saturn finger shows a greater capacity to deal with difficulties and limitations. However, the person may tend to worry too much or may take on more responsibility than is necessary and accept other people's burdens. Other indications are thoughtfulness and caution. Slowness may also become something of a problem.

A short Saturn finger can suggest a non-conformist with a

relaxed attitude to life. It can indicate a lack of responsibility and difficulty in dealing with problems, serious and minor. This may show up if the Saturn finger leans toward the ring, or Sun, finger, for such a person only wants a good time.

Another reading of the Saturn finger links it to the sex drive and religion. The connection between sexuality and religious awareness has been seen for thousands of years. The two derive from the same life energy channelled in different directions.

A strong Saturn finger will indicate a powerful libido. If the top phalanx appears more developed, the energy will emerge as a religious impulse. If the bottom one dominates, it will show up in the person's sex drive. A developed middle phalanx may indicate sublimation into more analytical, objective activities.

The Apollo or Sun Finger: In Greek myth Apollo, the Sun god, ruled the arts. The Apollo finger symbolizes the sunny side of life and a person's attitude to artistic work and appreciation. The average Apollo finger is about the same length as the Jupiter – halfway up the top phalanx of the Saturn finger.

At the simplest level a well-developed Apollo finger can signify optimism and a sunshiny attitude to life. Too strong, it may lead to problems in handling setbacks. A short Sun finger, however, can denote pessimism, the person who sees only the clouds and never the silver lining.

With regard to creativity, a long Apollo finger shows creative power and involvement with the arts. The longer the finger, the more pressing the creative urge and the need to express oneself. Whether success comes depends on other factors such as the Mercury finger, for instance; which represents money. The average Apollo finger indicates a subject who expresses him or herself creatively but in a more day-to-day manner without that push into art. A short Apollo finger does not mean that the subject lacks the creative impulse. It does, however, signify a block in expressing creativity. The person may adapt too much to outer realities, thereby cutting off the connection with the imagination.

The Apollo finger also shows an individual's way of appreciating the arts. This depends on the phalanges. The bottom phalanx indicates the sensual approach and a feeling for the beautiful. If the middle phalanx dominates, then the person will look at art more objectively, with a critical interest in the problems and challenges of creative work. The top phalanx signifies a concern for the spiritual values expressed in art – what the work means. If the phalanges appear balanced on a strong Apollo finger, the subject can work well in the arts, especially if the finger shows a square tip, for squareness indicates dexterity and, therefore, a good feel for technique.

The Mercury Finger: The average little finger reaches to the line between the top and middle phalanges of the ring finger. Sometimes, however, this finger begins low on the hand (below the curve formed by the base of the other fingers) so take this into account before judging its length.

The Mercury finger deals with two primary areas. The first is self-expression, particularly verbal expression. The second is money. The connection between these has led some palmists to look at a developed Mercury finger as the sign of a shady businessman, even a swindler. Indeed, in classical mythology, Mercury was the patron of thieves as well as of magicians and jugglers. We can also see it, however, as signifying a salesman or someone who succeeds through persuasion.

A long Mercury finger indicates a verbal person, who can convince others through argument and reason. This ability leads to self-confidence. A short Mercury finger can signify a sense of inferiority, especially when communicating ideas and feelings. This person may keep his or her ideas and feelings inside, or, on the other hand, may put things very bluntly, without tact. A long Mercury finger, however, can show a person who allows eloquence to slide into conceit, or even someone who manipulates others through words. The average Mercury finger will balance these qualities.

A long little finger also indicates the ability to make money. If it is short, the person may have to struggle financially or may find it hard to get the right job. An average little finger shows security but without that innate ability to amass a fortune. If bent, the Mercury finger can signify some sort of problem in dealing with financial matters. A lean towards the Apollo finger traditionally means someone who saves his or her money. It may also indicate a job in the financial side of the arts, as an agent perhaps or a promoter.

The Thumb (see Figure 9)*:* An opposable thumb sets us apart from almost all other animals. Significantly, a baby will unfold its thumb before any of the other fingers. It should not surprise us, therefore, that the thumb signifies that other aspect which distinguishes man from beast – the mind. The top phalanx, the spiritual level, represents the will. Even if will shows itself in such ordinary ways as determination and stubbornness, it allows us to transform ourselves from creatures of habit into spiritual beings. The second level, the mental level, represents reason and rationality, those qualities which allow us to comprehend the outside world.

Unlike the other fingers, the third phalanx does not form part of the thumb itself but rather the large, fleshy area beneath it, called the mount of Venus. We will look at all the mounts in a moment but here we should consider Venus's relation to the rest of the thumb. In general, the third phalanx represents the physical aspect of the personality. In other words, it signifies vitality, energy, and especially the sex drive.

To study the thumb we must first determine its placement, size, and length. First, the placement. Ask the subject to hold his or her fingers out straight and then close the thumb against the first finger (see Figure 10). The bottom of the fold will normally appear about halfway down the back of the mount of Venus. If higher, we refer to the thumb as placed high on the palm; if lower, we refer to it as placed low.

A highly placed thumb may indicate lack of adaptability, a closed mind, or a selfish quality. The person may take a rigid stance and believe him or herself to be infallible. A low-placed thumb can go too far in the opposite direction, signifying someone who is overly generous and easily swayed by the opinions of others.

The subject should then open the thumb while still keeping the fingers together. Notice the angle between the thumb and the Jupiter (index) finger (see Figure 11). This angle denotes thrift but also independence of thought. If the angle appears wide, more than 90 degrees, then the he or she will have a carefree attitude to money, spending or giving it freely. It may also indicate that the person follows her or his own course mentally, never simply adopting someone else's ideas, even if those ideas are worth while.

An angle of between 60 and 90 degrees is considered normal. In terms of thrift, the person will show more caution with money but can also let go of it when necessary. Other factors may push him or her either to miserliness or generosity. Similarly, the subject will have independence of thought but may well follow others if the circumstances seem right.

A narrow angle shows a tendency to hang on tightly to money. You might discuss this with the person for, if it becomes a problem, he or she may wish to curb this inclination. A narrow angle also suggests a follower, someone who has trouble developing their own view of things.

Next, check the length and thickness of the thumb. The average thumb reaches a length slightly less than that of the little finger. Another method of checking length involves closing the thumb against the side of the first finger. A thumb of average length will reach halfway up the bottom phalanx. In width the average thumb measures about one and a quarter times that of the widest finger. A narrow, short thumb may indicate a person who has difficulty in achieving his or her goals and who finds it hard to impose his or her will on the world. A long, wide thumb suggests someone with a strong success impulse. This does not

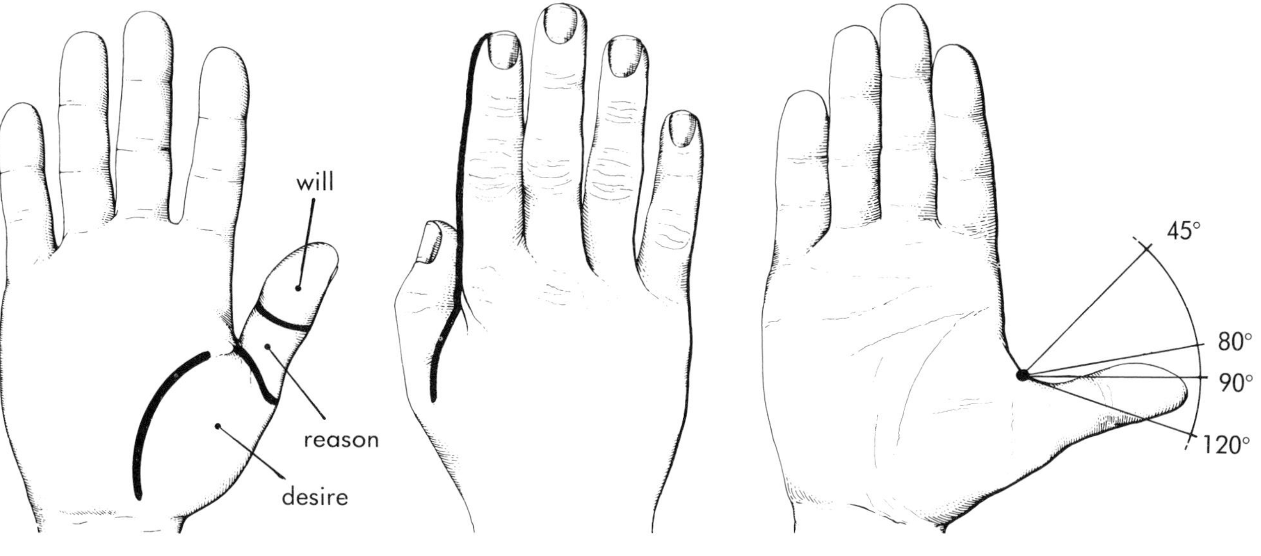

Figure 9.
Thumb phalanges including the mount of Venus

Figure 10.
Placement of the thumb seen from the back of the hand

Figure 11.
Angles of the thumb

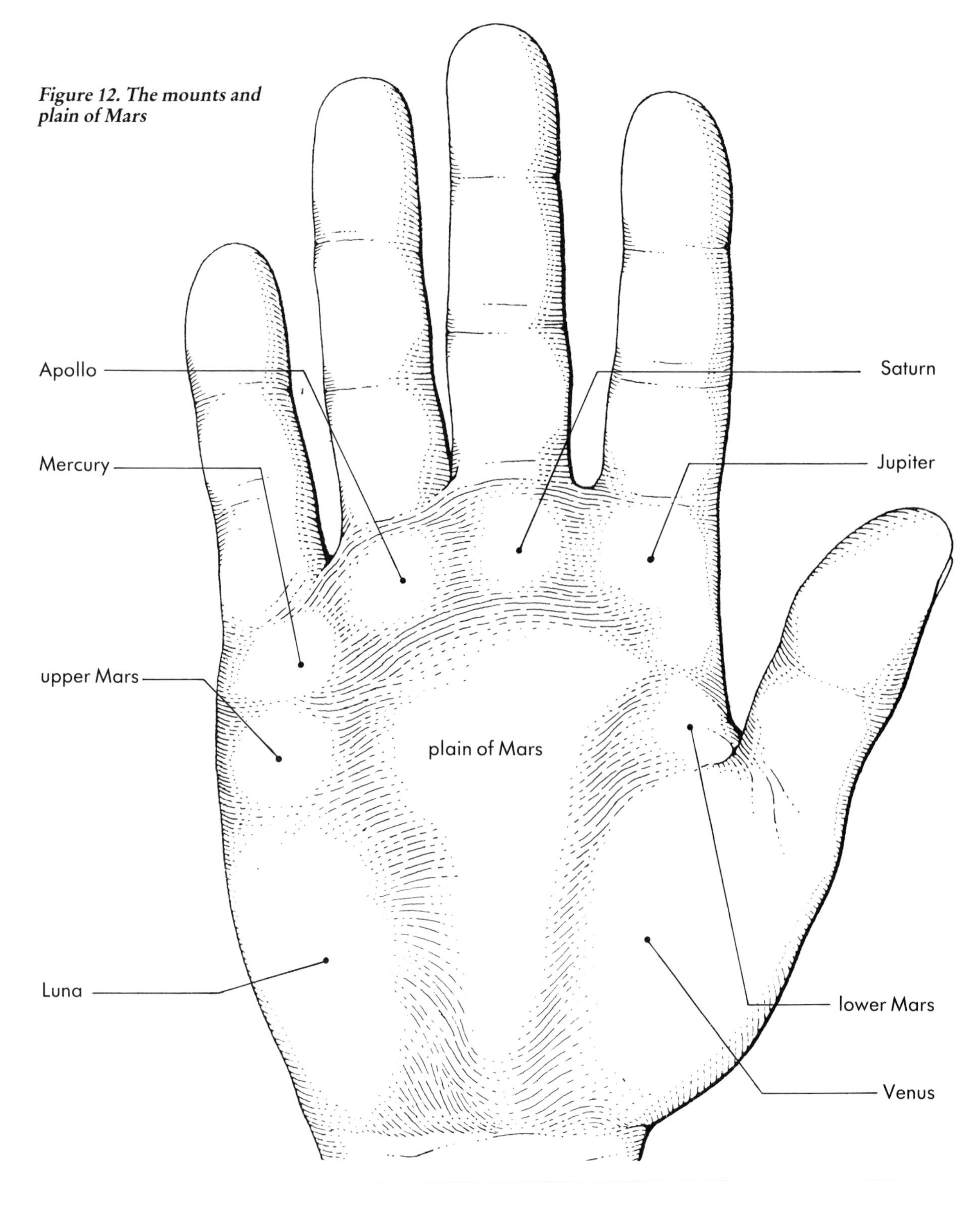

Figure 12. The mounts and plain of Mars

mean that a short thumb signifies failure. Rather it shows someone who finds it harder to drive him or herself to overcome obstacles.

As with the fingers, the thumb's phalanges have different meanings. The average thumb has the first phalanx two-thirds the length of the second phalanx. Thus, a long first phalanx would measure almost the same length as the second. Besides being of varying length, one phalanx may appear noticeably thicker than another. If the top phalanx dominates, then the will overpowers the reason and the person will go after what he or she wants without spending much time in thinking things out. If the second appears longer and thicker, he or she will analyse everything to the point of inaction.

Particular thumb shapes have certain meanings. A clubbed thumb, where the first phalanx is wide, rounded, and thick, suggests a tendency to violent temper. Whether this manifests itself or not will depend on other factors in the hand. A flattened thumb is indicative of low vitality and the person will need to conserve energy.

If the second phalanx narrows after the joint we call this 'waisted'. It denotes a strong intuitive sense. A line across the second phalanx near the joint with the top indicates temper. A line further down shows stubbornness. We can understand this if we remember that the middle phalanx represents reason. Both temper and stubbornness cut through rationality.

The tops of some thumbs bend back, often quite far. According to some palmists, this indicates someone who is easily persuaded. I have found that it can signify a person whose willpower does not depend on the submission of others. The will directs itself to achieving what it wishes without regarding other people as opponents or competitors.

THE MOUNTS

The term 'mount' refers to the raised, fleshy parts of the hand (see Figure 12). Some mounts are more prominent than others, indicating strength in those aspects of life the mount represents. A 'good' mount is one in which the raised portion is firm but not overtly hard. Very high, however, and it signifies excess in the relevant area.

We will begin with the mounts under the fingers. All the mounts represent qualities of basic energy. The finger mounts, therefore, indicate the energy used by that finger. In other words, a developed Apollo finger indicates involvement with the arts. But the finger will need a good mount to give it the energy to make something out of that involvement. A good mount under a finger shows not only the presence but also the development of the energy related to the finger. Sometimes the mount appears flat but vertical lines will run below the finger towards the palm. These can substitute for a raised mount. They may indicate that the person has developed a particular quality rather than inheriting it. An aquaintance of mine writes about religion. One would expect her to have strong mounts of Apollo (art) and Saturn (religion). Neither stands out in her hand; however, marked lines run from both fingers to the heart line.

The Mount of Jupiter: A good mount of Jupiter indicates a leader, someone who gets along easily with others and who demonstrates self-assurance and enjoyment of life – in short, the kind of person we call 'jovial' (Jove was another name for Jupiter). A low Jupiter mount (especially when coupled with a weak Jupiter finger) indicates diffidence, perhaps a negative attitude to life and its possibilities. People with this problem can work consciously to overcome their pessimism or sense of inferiority.

The Mount of Saturn: Saturn, remember, deals with life's difficulties. A good mount here shows a person who deals with setbacks in a positive way, taking Saturn-like problems as learning experiences. As Saturn also represents religion, a developed Saturn mount may also denote someone with a strong religious sense. A low mount would indicate the lack of these qualities and may also indicate someone who tends to withdraw from others, especially when faced with problems. In spiritual terms it may signify a solitary approach to religion. Many people associate Saturn with the Tarot image of the Hermit.

The Mount of Apollo: The mount of Apollo shows artistic leanings. Some palmists stress the creative side of Apollo, while others feel that it signifies material success. An overly developed or puffy mount of Apollo indicates someone given to daydreams and visions without the discipline to bring them to fruition.

The Mount of Mercury: The mount of Mercury indicates a good business sense. High development signifies ambition and skill in financial negotiations. A very high mount, with a long Mercury finger (especially with a long second phalanx), may signify the conman quality often associated with Mercury. A low mount may mean limited ambition or simply a lack of interest in the business world. Mercury also shows communication skills and sometimes a talent for medicine or the occult. All these qualities traditionally belong to Mercury, known variously as the god of doctors, magicians, scientists, businessmen, and thieves. To find out which area applies, look for other signs in the hand and tactfully discuss the possibilities with the subject.

The Mount of Venus: The mount of Venus forms the third phalanx of the thumb. On many hands the life line will encircle the mount (although the top part of the circle belongs to the lower mount of Mars). This mount represents vitality and, in particular, sexual vitality. On the simplest level, a well-developed mount of Venus indicates someone with a strong sex drive and a great interest in sexual relationships. A flat mount denotes someone who does not find sex so important. If we regard sexuality as basic life energy, then a good mount of Venus characterizes someone who enjoys life. We can think of this mount as supplying energy to the thumb. The thumb shows will and reason but both require an underpinning of vitality.

We can also see this mount as describing a person's emotional relations in general. In this context a developed and firm mount shows someone who gets along well with others and who enjoys and values emotional connections. An overdeveloped mount, which is high, somewhat puffy, and perhaps brightly coloured, would then indicate someone who takes emotions too seriously. Such a person forms very intense relationships. If expressed sexually, this mount denotes someone very aggressive and demanding whose sexual needs dominate his or her life. The palmist can, of course, discuss these possibilities with the subject but sex is one of those areas where the diviner needs to apply a good measure of tact.

The Mount of Luna (The Moon Mount): The Moon mount appears on the hand opposite the mount of Venus. Traditionally, the Moon rules the unconscious, the hidden side of life. The unconscious reveals itself to us through the imagination, so a developed mount of Luna signifies a powerful imagination. Combined with such factors as a strong Apollo finger, it may indicate creative talent, particularly in writing. The mount itself shows the action of the imagination. Flat, it reveals someone very down to earth who judges life in terms of the 'real world'. Very high, it can indicate not only visionary or psychic abilities but also mental disturbance, since the Moon brings out both these sides of the unconscious. If the mount of Luna merges with the mount of upper Mars, this implies a determination to do something with the imagination. For a writer or an artist it can indicate discipline.

The Mounts of Mars: In classical mythology Mars was the god of war. The two mounts of Mars, however, do not signify violence so much as courage and determination. Many palmists see the hand as divided into an active and a passive side. The dividing line runs down the middle of the Saturn finger to between the mounts of Venus and Luna. The side by the thumb, symbol of the mind, is active. The outside half of the hand, which includes Luna, symbol of the unconscious, is passive.

Upper Mars falls on the passive part of the hand. It comes in between the heart line and the end (or the extension) of the head line or alternatively, in between the mount of Luna and the mount of Mercury. Upper Mars signifies passive courage and the ability to endure. Well-developed, it shows determination and someone who does not give in to pressure. This is not the courage to conquer or take the initiative but rather the courage to keep going. A flat mount here means the person will need to cultivate such qualities to avoid abandoning goals when faced by obstacles.

Lower Mars, in between the mount of Venus and the curve of the life line, falls on the active side of the hand. So it shows active courage, the ability to tackle a difficult situation. This can denote courage to begin new things as well as bravery in a fight or a crisis. Some people see this mount as demonstrating physical courage in particular, interpreting an overly developed lower Mars as signifying a tendency to violence. Looked at in a broader context, we can say that a very high mount of lower Mars will show aggression and perhaps a tendency to view life and relationships in terms of battle.

Compare the two mounts of Mars. If the lower appears noticeably higher than the upper, the person will show courage in beginning projects but will find it difficult to continue after the first push. If the upper dominates, then the subject may show great endurance but a reluctance to take the initiative or break old patterns.

Plain of Mars: The area in the centre of the hand, the hollow, is called the plain of Mars. For most people this area will appear concave. If it is slightly raised or even if it is flat, we call it high. Only if very indented, do we call it low. The plain shows sensitivity. Very high, it will signify someone overbearing and proud with little tact or awareness of the problems of others. Very low, it can indicate someone overly sensitive to the opinions of others and that person may feel other people's pain very personally.

If you feel the subject's palm, you will notice whether or not the centre feels firm or soft. This quality acts as another indicator of basic vitality. A firm plain of Mars shows someone with good reserves of energy. If it is too hard, however, this can suggest a refusal to adapt to change or new situations.

LINES AND MARKINGS

Hold your hand in front of you with the fingers extended and the palm facing you. Now slowly bend the fingers forward and curl the palm in upon itself. Do this a couple of times. Notice the way the flesh settles into the same creases each time. These creases form the lines which we study to understand character and experience.

THE PRINCIPAL LINES

The lines give us a record of the past and of the potential that the future holds. By comparing the lines in the major and minor hands (see Figure 13), we can see what a subject has done with the possibilities given by life. The three principal lines – life, head, and heart – appear quite early on, while the subject is still a baby (although they will change as he or she gets older). For this reason some palmists read them as a genetic record, or even an indication of past lives. The novice palmist would probably do best to concentrate on what they tell us about this life.

Before examining the lines individually, we should consider the different markings that may appear on each of them (see Figure 14). In general, the markings show some sort of block or diversion. Bars and dots signify interruptions or hindrances. A cross will show a more significant or longer lasting problem. A square, however, represents protection and good health. Chains indicate confusion and a spreading of energy. The heart line, however, is usually chained, for few people focus their emotions very sharply. An island on a line means that energy temporarily diverges in two directions before returning. A tassel at the end of the line shows a scattering of the line's power. A fork

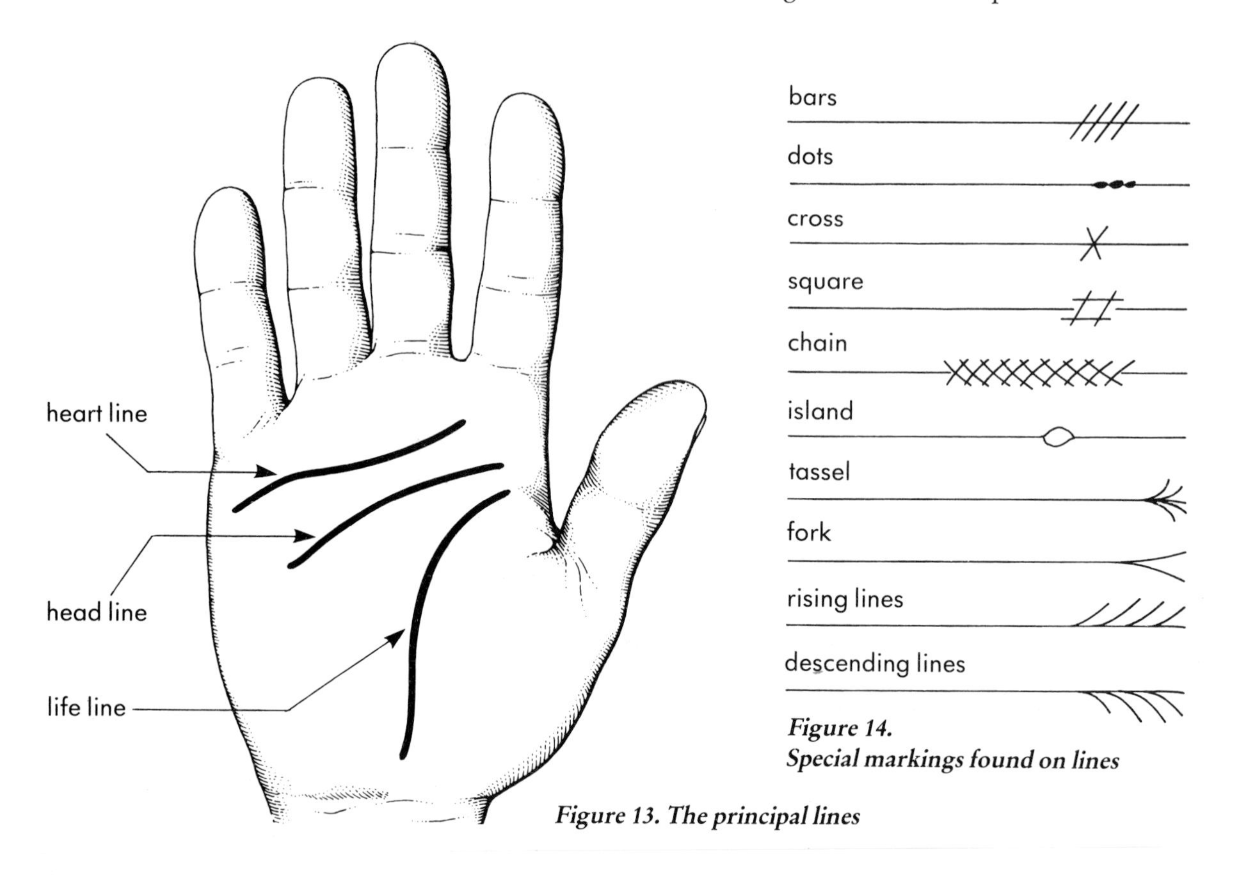

Figure 14.
Special markings found on lines

Figure 13. The principal lines

increases a person's possibilities. Branches may help or hinder the line, depending on whether they branch up towards the fingers or down towards the wrist.

The Life Line: People often ask palmists how long they will live. Unfortunately, many palmists will attempt to answer them. A short life line does not, however, indicate a short life. Any responsible palmist will say firmly that such a prediction is impossible.

The life line begins at the edge of the hand in between the thumb and the mount of Jupiter. It swings around the mounts of Mars and Venus, usually ending at the bottom of the hand, sometimes stopping before that point, sometimes continuing around to the end of the wrist. Often the life line begins joined to the head line.

An early divergence of the head and life lines indicates an early separation from parental influence. If the two do not touch at all, the person knew his or her own mind even as an infant. If the life line begins high on the hand, it indicates self-confidence. A wide arc shows someone who likes people and feels at ease in company. A narrow arc denotes shyness, or simply a preference for being alone.

A short life line, especially if it appears faint, indicates a weak constitution, as well as potential health problems. A life line which gets fainter at the end can signify ill health in old age. If weaker, or broken, at the beginning, ask the person about childhood illnesses or accidents. A long and deeply etched life line represents health and vitality.

Sometimes the life line appears in two parts, usually with the second half in a wider or narrower arc than the first (see Figure 15). This denotes a break with past experience and the start of a new way of life. If the second arc swings more widely than the first, it signifies a life that becomes freer, more individual and less conformist. A narrower second arc means a change to a more restricted life. If a blank space appears between the end of one arc and the start of the next, this can signify a crisis or illness which results in the changes implied by the two arcs.

Discussing such things as crises and changes raises the question of dating events on the lines. Experienced palmists sometimes judge time from the head or heart lines but the

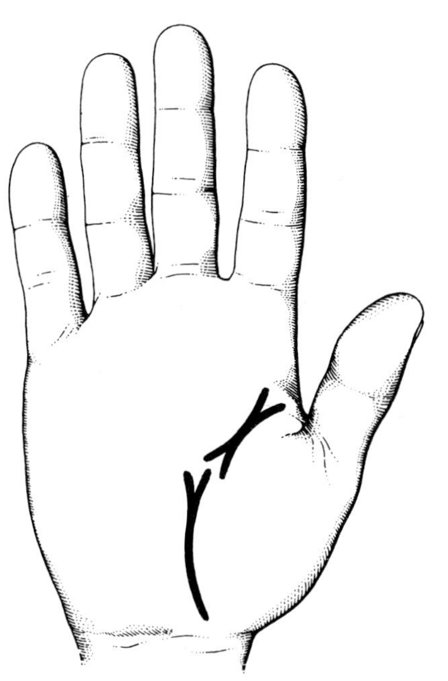

Figure 15. Break in the life line showing branches

majority find the life line the most dependable. The simplest method regards the halfway point of the life line as the midpoint of someone's life. Distance can then be estimated before and after. Another method of finding the midpoint is to draw a line from the mount of Saturn to the centre of the mount of Venus. The midpoint is where this line intersects the life line. If the life line is longer before this point, then the person's early experiences shaped her or his character very strongly. If longer after this point, then later life is more significant.

For a more detailed approach, draw lines from the centre of the mount of Venus to the centre of each of the finger mounts, the mounts of upper Mars and Luna, and the centre of the wrist lines (see Figure 16). The points where these lines cross the life line represent the years as follows: ten, twenty, thirty, forty, fifty, sixty-five, and eighty.

Notice that this method assumes, firstly, a life line of average length and, secondly, a life line that continues around the hand. As you work more with palmistry you will develop your own methods for dating events.

Branches reaching up from the life line towards the fingers indicate special aptitudes, depending on the finger. A branch towards Jupiter shows ambition, usually crowned by success. A branch towards Apollo denotes good fortune, to Saturn determination, to Mercury mental ability and financial aptitude. Multiple branches indicate combined abilities and interests. If the lines branch from different points on the life line, this can suggest various major concerns at different times in the subject's life. In other words, a branch high on the life line towards Apollo would show an early interest in the arts. A branch lower down towards Mercury would reveal that later in life the focus had changed from the arts to business.

While looking at the life line, remember to check any markings for signs of difficulty, interruptions or protection. Also, compare the two hands. A weak life line on the minor hand and a strong one on the major shows that the person has developed a stronger sense of self. It is also indicative of increased vitality. A stronger life line on the minor hand suggests that the subject could do more with his or her life. It may indicate as well that he or she has dissipated good health through bad habits.

The Head Line: Just as a short life line does not denote a short life, so a short head line does not signify low intelligence. A short line shows a narrow yet focused range of interest but, if it appears faint and narrow, then it implies a lack of concentration. A deep head line indicates a love of learning. A break, or markings, may show blocks or breaks in education.

The head line usually begins either touching the life line or somewhere above it, below the mount of Jupiter. The line may end under the Apollo finger or under the mount of Mercury. Some head lines are straight, others dip down, some even reaching the mount of Luna.

A downward curve shows imagination; if it enters the mount of Luna it indicates a very powerful imagination. Fantasies may dominate the person's mental processes. A downward dip may suggest imaginative activity, especially with a strong Apollo finger. In contrast, a straight line into or towards the mount of Mars denotes practicality and common sense.

We have seen that a separated head and life line shows early independence. Widely separated, however, it can indicate impulsiveness. We can see the logic of this if we envisage the distinction between an individual's interests (head line) and needs (life line). By the same token, if the head line actually begins *inside* the heart line it reveals extreme carefulness, perhaps a defensive attitude to life or a desire for protection. These things may arise from an early trauma.

Branches reaching down from the head line indicate worries. Branches up show interest in whatever finger the branch reaches towards. A branch towards Jupiter would mean social interests, towards Saturn religious conviction, towards Apollo artistic interest, towards Mercury financial or communication skills.

Forks at the end of the head line show increased mental capacity and, in particular, the ability to work in two areas. If one fork dips down towards Luna and the other continues straight, it implies imagination coupled with common sense. This divergence may indicate a writer, especially if the fork towards Luna is longer.

Markings on the head line can sometimes point to physical or mental problems. Dots may mean headaches, crosses can indicate head injuries, an island nervous strain. Bars, however, may signify a break in education or career. Squares, as usual, mean protection from potential trouble, in this case anxieties. A chained head line indicates nervousness or timidity, especially in expressing ideas. It may also show a lack of conviction.

The Heart Line: Many people associate three questions with palmistry: how long they will live; when they will marry; and how many children they will have. Just as reputable palmists today do not attempt to answer the first question, so most will avoid the other two as well. The heart line does not show who you will marry although it does say a good deal about how you will behave in marriage and other romantic situations.

The heart line runs above the head line from the opposite direction. It begins under Mercury at the edge of the hand and ends at the mount of Jupiter. A strong heart line, ending not too high in Jupiter, well defined and without branches, indicates someone loyal in love, with steady emotions. A long line, rising to the top of the mount, shows a person who gives a great deal in love but expects at least as much in return.

The heart line may end in the area between the Jupiter and Saturn fingers instead of under Jupiter. This indicates a person who shows affection but who can also become rather passive. A line rising to between the fingers themselves can suggest problems with jealousy or an obsession.

If the line ends under Saturn it may mean that the person does not show much emotion. This trait can come from selfishness but it may also be the result of over-caution or a fear of getting hurt. The hidden emotions may be quite powerful, especially if the lines appear well formed. Once this person is emotionally committed, he or she can demonstrate great feeling and loyalty.

If the line curves upward the person will be demonstrative. A straight heart line indicates reserve, while one that dips down may signify coldness. A high heart line shows subjectivity, a low line better judgment in emotional and romantic matters but also a harsher, more judgmental attitude towards others.

A deep heart line usually signifies correspondingly deep emotions, even if the person does not show them openly. With a lighter line, he or she may display great feeling but some of this emotion may not be long lasting.

As mentioned above, the heart line commonly appears chained, a sign that most people express their emotions in

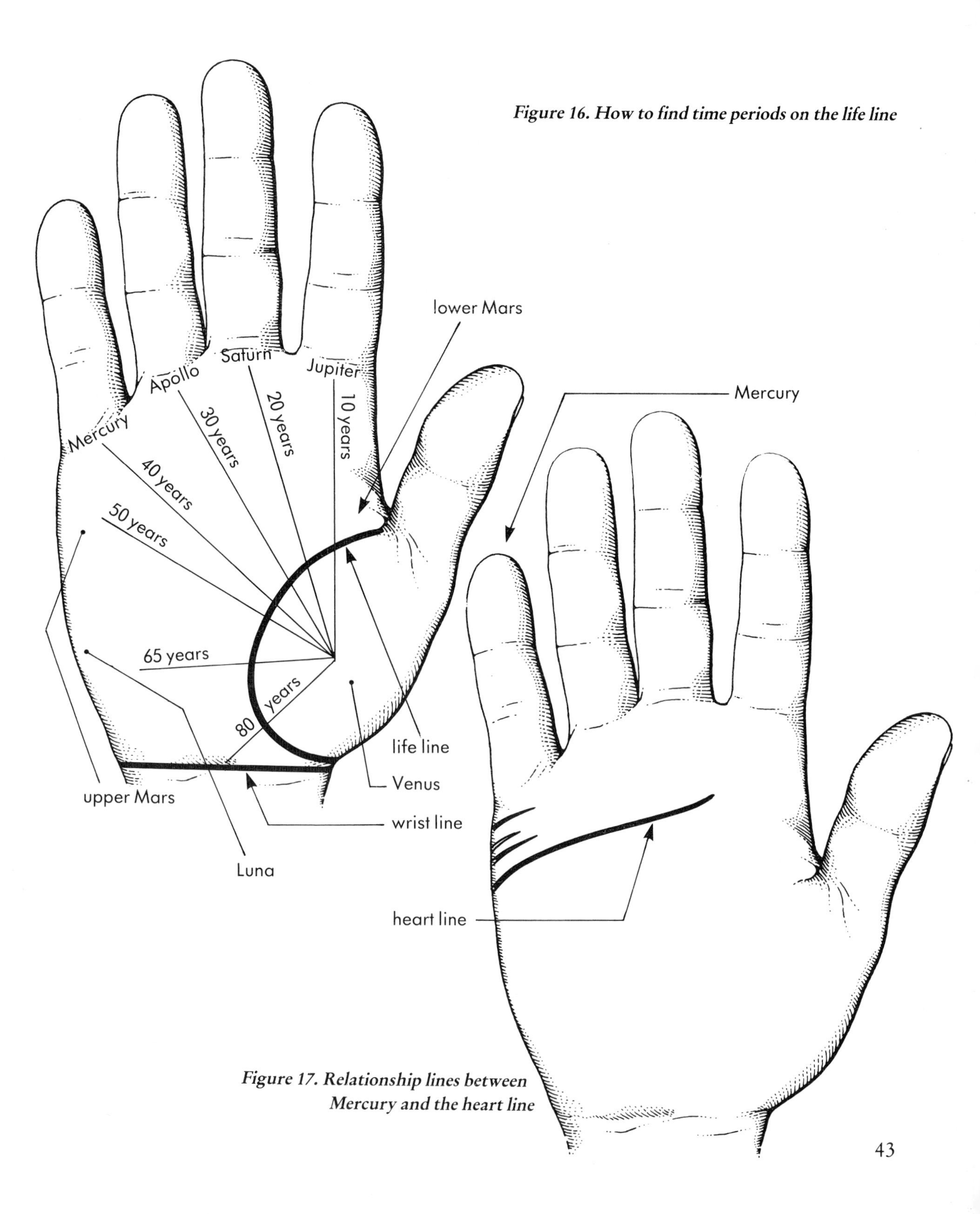

Figure 16. How to find time periods on the life line

Figure 17. Relationship lines between Mercury and the heart line

different ways depending on the person they are with. Very pronounced chains can mean extreme and unfocused emotion. The heart line will often appear forked at the end. This can indicate having to choose between different lovers. It also shows that as the person gets older his or her capacity for love increases. If the fork appears on the major hand only the concept of choice is increased.

The meaning of branches depends on whether they reach up towards the fingers or down towards the head line. Up indicates success in love and good relationships. Down suggests disappointments in love.

If down branches appear in the minor hand but not in the major, it may show that the person has learned to counteract tendencies that might cause relationships to go badly. A large number of short branches, especially at the beginning of the heart line, suggests either a flirt or someone who cares more for conquests than serious relationships.

For many people the heart line will also say something about the heart itself. As a general rule, the deeper and firmer the line appears, the stronger the heart. The usual markings – squares for protection, dots and bars for difficulties, and so on – will apply here as well. However, novice palmists should take great care in making any judgments about so vital an organ as the heart.

The markings will apply, too, to emotional questions. An island indicates an interruption in the emotional life, perhaps the end of a relationship with an interval before another is begun. A break in the heart line shows an emotional block, usually caused by a traumatic event of some sort. It may, however, appear more severe than it really is. Other signs in the hand can help to interpret the true meaning of this block.

Returning to the theme of marriage – or more properly, relationships, since marriage forms only one kind of strong bond between people – many hands will show one or more short lines, relationship lines, in between the little finger and the heart line (see Figure 17). These lines indicate the presence of important relationships in a person's life. A long, firm line will suggest a primary connection (such as a good marriage), while shorter lines above or below the primary line will show the presence of other significant relationships, such as romantic affairs and involvements.

THE MINOR LINES

While all hands will show the three principal lines, each hand will also exhibit a variety of others (see Figure 18). The experienced palmist will learn to recognize the different lines and combinations of them. Here, we will look briefly at three of the most common.

The Fate or Destiny Line: This line begins somewhere near the bottom of the hand and runs upwards towards the mount of Saturn. It does not show fate in the sense of preordained events but depicts a subject's ability to find his or her path in life. More

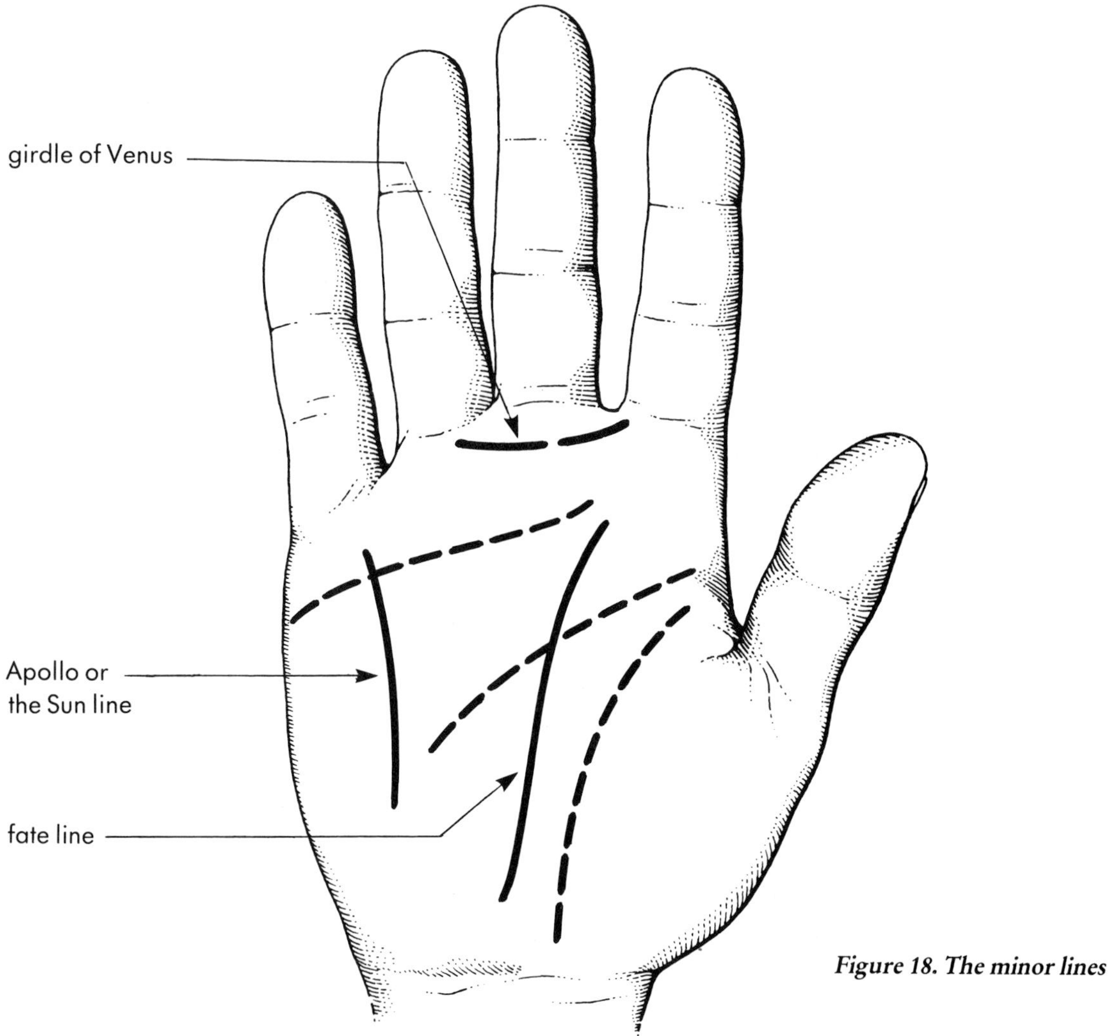

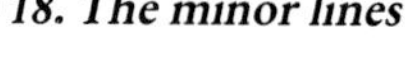
Figure 18. The minor lines

specifically, it can show a person establishing a career. As mentioned above, the absence of this line does not imply disaster or a weak person but is indicative of someone who has gone his or her own way. It may also describe someone with different ideas and attitudes from those of society.

In general, a low fate line indicates early ambition. Continuing high up the hand it shows freedom of choice. A long and strongly etched fate line denotes a person with a sense of destiny and self-worth. If the fate line ends abruptly at the head line it shows a lack of ambition, especially later in life. The person will have to overcome a tendency to accept a role that has been defined early on. If the line shifts at some point, especially after the head line, it indicates a career break or a fresh start in life. If it starts around or after the head line it means that something will stimulate ambition relatively late in life. A fate line that ends at the heart line implies ambition blocked by emotional relationships. A partner may create obstacles to the subject's goals. A fate line that begins in Luna shows someone who takes a path which brings public approval, often leading to success.

If deep, the fate line shows a determined approach to marking out a path and achieving objectives. Uneven depth along the fate line indicates a wavering sense of purpose in life.

The Sun Line (Line of Apollo): The true Sun line ends either at the mount of Apollo or else heads clearly in that direction. It may start low in the hand, from the mount of Luna, it may begin at the head line, or even in the mount of Apollo itself.

The Sun line implies the presence of talent together with a likelihood of success. It does not describe the kind of talent; other aspects of the hand, such as the fingers and mounts, do this. The lack of a Sun line is not indicative of failure. Many people's hands do not contain this line and there are plenty of other indications in the hand which may compensate for this lack. It may, however, show a person who does not look for outer achievements but who finds their private life more important.

The length of the Sun line indicates various aspects of success. To judge the strength of the line we look not at length but at depth and clarity. If the line appears very clear then the person will probably succeed. A deep line suggests a good deal of talent, along with the desire to express it. A long Sun line may show early success. One that begins higher up, after the head line, can indicate a longer wait for recognition but can also signify that the person succeeds without much outside assistance. These two interpretations may often combine, for a person who gets no help from other sources will often take longer to succeed but may appreciate his or her success more.

A break in the Sun line indicates a change of direction at some time in life, quite possibly a change in career. Two or more Sun lines represent a variety of interests. Other features in the hand will reveal whether or not the person balances these multiple interests well or allows them to drain off energy.

The Girdle of Venus: This is a less common sign. Expressed most fully it shows up as a semicircle running from between the fingers of Jupiter and Saturn to between the fingers of Apollo and Mercury. More often, it appears fragmented or does not run all the way across. The girdle indicates both sensitivity and a need for sensual excitement and satisfaction. A very pronounced girdle of Venus – long and clearly marked – shows a person who feels strongly for others and who displays love and emotion. It also denotes someone with a large appetite for stimulation and gratification. This does not refer only to sex. The person may seek stimulation in powerful relationships or adventure. He or she may create situations that provoke strong reactions. Still, with a strong girdle of Venus sex will be a primary drive.

A less pronounced girdle of Venus – a smaller semicircle, for instance – will indicate that these qualities are balanced by a sense of moderation and more rational judgment. A large but broken girdle of Venus can indicate conflict between restraint and the desire for gratification.

The Quadrangle: This marking is not a line but rather the space between the head line and the heart line. A quadrangle of average width (experience will help you judge the average) with only a slight narrowing in the centre and roughly the same opening at both ends, indicates a balanced person, someone with an even temper who is independent, yet open to the influence of others. The slight narrowing shows that the person is not inflexible, either emotionally (the heart line) or rationally

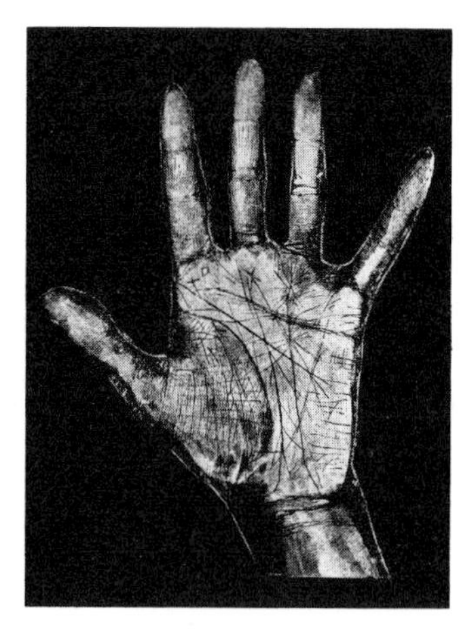

The left hand of Sarah Bernhardt, the late nineteenth-century actress. The spatulate hand shape shows someone unconventional, needing mental stimulation. She is hard-working, demanding great effort from others. The pointed fingertips (especially Jupiter and Mercury) show a desire to communicate. The long Mercury finger denotes great persuasive power. The waisted thumb shows intuition, the long Apollo finger artistic interest.

Notice the long, deep life line, indicating vitality. The head line drives straight down into Luna, denoting a dominant imagination. The separated life line and head line signify life-long independence. There are two crosses, under Jupiter and Saturn, indicating sexual difficulties, and conflict in leadership. The square next to the Jupiter cross shows protection – the conflicts will not seriously harm her.

(the head line). If either line doesn't bend at all it suggests rigidity. If the quadrangle narrows considerably in the centre, this may show weakness, or susceptibility to others. If the head line dips, the person lacks confidence in his or her ideas. If the heart line drops, the weakness appears emotionally. A waisted quadrangle may also signify some difficulty in mid-life.

A narrow quadrangle shows someone relatively closed to others. He or she does not allow much space between thought and emotion for people to enter and influence his or her life. A very wide quadrangle denotes a gullible person who needs more protection from outside influences. If the quadrangle opens more widely on the side of the thumb, it indicates someone nervous about stating an opinion. If it opens towards the edge of the hand, it signifies frankness. A very wide opening towards the edge can suggest bluntness and pugnacious self-expression.

There are many more lines, markings, and other signs in the hand. In time you will learn to recognize them and comprehend their meanings. Remember that no single indication will reveal everything about a person. To read a hand means balancing all the elements until a whole picture emerges.

FURTHER STUDY

The information given here will enable you to begin reading hands. As you become more practised you will probably want to consult other books or take courses. These will increase your knowledge of particular lines and markings. Experience, however, is at least as important. Begin with your own hand and the hands of people you know fairly well. That way, you can compare the indications you find in the hand with what you already know about the person. When consulting books, try to think of how the general descriptions might fit specific cases and to understand the way in which one sign combines with or modifies another.

Be careful about interpreting weaknesses or barriers. Try to look at blocks in a positive way. Remember that we create our own lives from the possibilities given to us.

You may wish to make prints of your own or other people's hands (see Figure 19) to study them more carefully. The photocopier has greatly aided the palmist. Lay the palm down on the glass and cover it with a white cloth to block out any extraneous light. Let the hand's own weight anchor it on the glass. Do the backs of the hands as well as the palms and label them as right and left.

You can also get a good print, at least of the palm, by using printer's ink and good quality paper. Place the paper over a sheet of relatively soft rubber and plastic. With a roller rub ink on the palm, then press the hand down firmly but without sliding. Roll the hand off the paper, beginning at the wrist. You may need to experiment a few times but this method gives a clear picture of the mounts and contours as well as the lines.

Making hand prints serves another purpose. If you date them and look at the hand some time later – better still, make successive prints at various intervals – you will get a clearer sense of the way hands alter, mirroring the changes in people's lives.

Figure 19. Prints of the left and right palms, showing differences between the major and minor hands

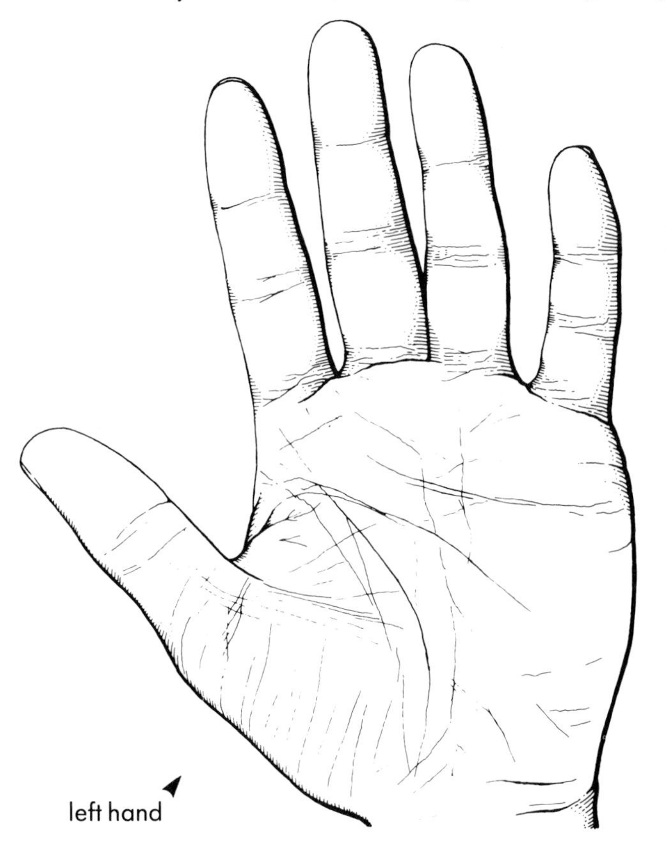

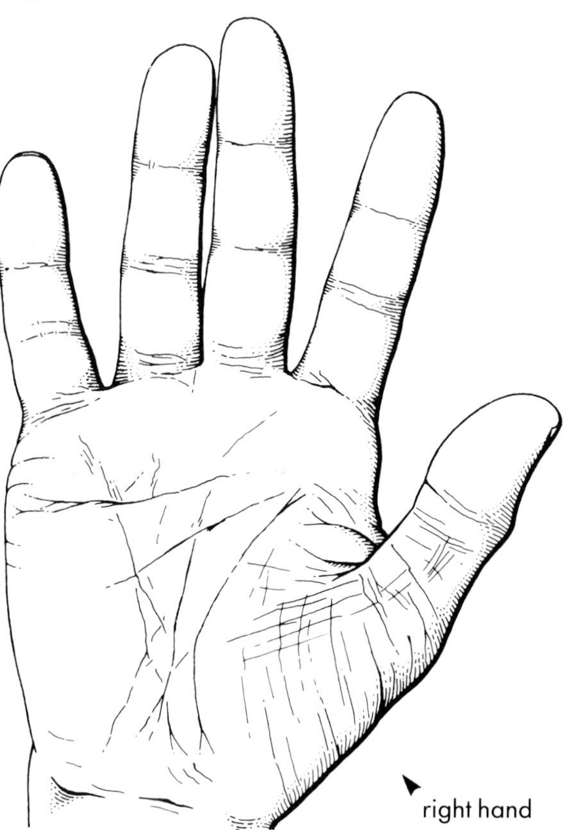

TEA LEAVES

Tea leaf reading, properly called tasseography, belongs to the vast range of divination methods involving images and symbols. As mentioned in the Introduction, people have watched the way ashes fall from a fire, have thrown pebbles into the dust and seen the patterns they formed, and have examined the entrails of slaughtered animals. In all of these methods – and in tasseography – the diviner detects a sign in the bits and pieces and then interprets that sign symbolically. The technique for creating a reading out of tea leaves is very simple. Interpretation, however, may take some practice, for it requires the diviner first to recognize the images, second to interpret the meaning of each one, and third, to combine the different symbols into a coherent message. All of these steps require both imagination and intuition. Imagination allows the reader to see the possibilities, while intuition points the way to a true interpretation.

You can use coffee grounds as well as tea leaves. In both cases, choose a white cup with no inside pattern or decoration. The subject of the reading should drink the tea or coffee, leaving a small amount of liquid. Holding the cup in the left hand, he or she should swirl the liquid three times clockwise, trying to make sure that the leaves (or grounds) are carried up to the rim of the cup without spilling over it. The subject then inverts the cup into the saucer, holding it for a count of seven to allow the liquid to drain away. When the cup is turned right side up again the reader can examine and interpret the images created. The handle of the cup should point towards the reader.

Many leaves imply a full life just as many specific images suggest several issues important to the person. If their meanings contradict, then the subject is confused or undecided. Larger images, however, will show more powerful influences and this distinction may help him or her make decisions. In general, dots will emphasize a sign's importance as will the image of a finger pointing at a sign.

Some readers consider signs on the left of the handle as denoting the past and on the right as the future. More commonly, the signs near the rim of the cup refer to the present or near future, while those towards the bottom refer to the past. For some specific signs the top is considered lucky, the bottom unlucky.

These general rules will help you gain a sense of what the signs mean. A genuine interpretation, however, depends on allowing the images to stimulate your perceptions. Now and then a very

A Victorian photograph showing divining by the cup. Reading the shapes made by tea leaves or coffee grounds requires some practice by the diviner who must, first, recognize the images, then interpret their meanings and finally, combine the different symbols into a coherent message.

clear picture will emerge. More often, you will need to discover the sign within a clump of tea leaves (see Figures 20-23). The same goes for meanings. You will need imagination not just to see the image but to understand what it can mean for a particular person in a specific situation at a specific time.

Below, you will find a list of traditional meanings for signs in tasseography. Remember that these *are* traditional and not fixed. Usually they derive from logic. A sword means an argument, a chair means a guest, jewels mean gifts, and so on. You can apply similar logic to the signs you discover in the cup. For each person the true meaning of a symbol lies within the mind's ability to perceive it and then to connect it with life and experience.

acorn – at the top, success and gain; at the bottom, good health
aircraft – journey; if broken, danger of accident; can mean rise in position
anchor – rest, stability, constancy; clouded, inconstancy
apple – achievement
axe – difficulties; near top, overcome
baby – small worries
bag – a trap; if open, escape
ball – variable fortunes
bell – unexpected news; good if near top
birds – good news
boat – visit from friend, protection
book – open, good news; closed, need to investigate something
bush – new friends or opportunities; something growing in life
butterfly – fickleness
cabbage – jealousy; with dots, at work
candle – help from others
cap – trouble, take care
cat – deceit, a false friend
chain – engagement, a wedding
chair – a guest
cigar – new friends
circle – success, completion; with a dot, a baby
clock – better health
clouds – trouble; with dots, many problems
coin – money coming
comb – an enemy
cross – suffering, sacrifice
cup – reward
dagger – danger from self or others, beware of recklessness
dish – trouble at home
dog – good friend; if at bottom, friend needs help
door – odd event

Figure 20. Tea leaves depicting a circle, a lion, a cross and a ship

Figure 21. Tea leaves depicting a tree, a ring, a snake and a forked line

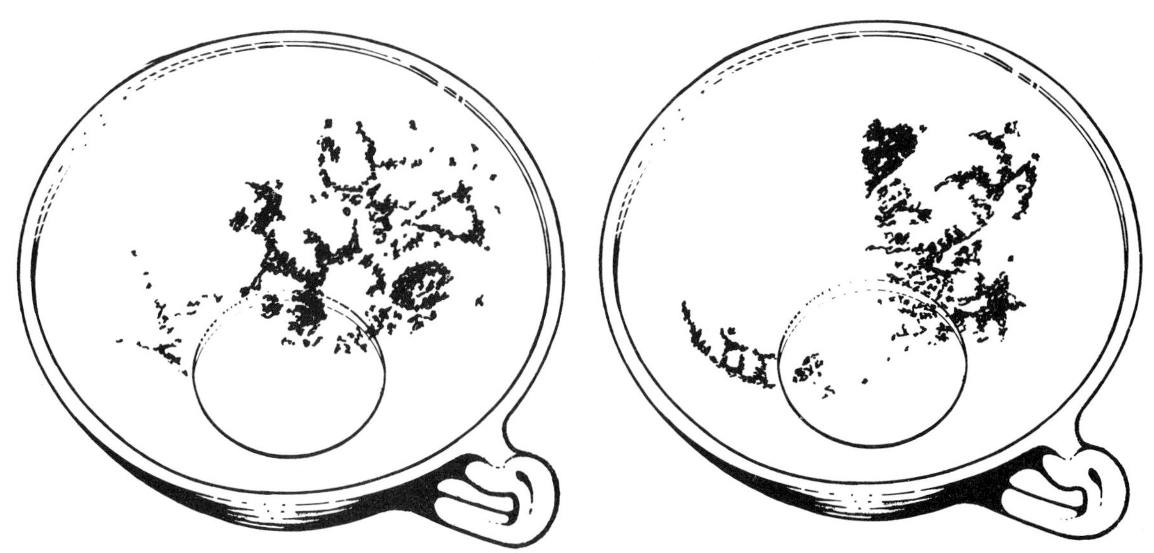

Figure 22. Tea leaves depicting a triangle, a dog, a horseshoe and an egg

Figure 23. Tea leaves depicting a heart, a star, a ladder and a palm tree

Recognizing different shapes

duck – money coming
egg – good omen
elephant – wisdom and strength
envelope – good news
eye – caution
face – a change, may be a setback
fan – flirtation
feather – lack of concentration
fence – limitations, minor setbacks, not permanent
finger – emphasizes whatever sign it points at
fire – achievement, especially artistic; danger of haste
fish – good fortune
flag – danger
fly – domestic annoyance
fork – false flattery
forked line – decision
fruit – prosperity
gate – opportunity, future success
glass – integrity
glow – a challenge
goat – be careful of enemies
grapes – happiness
gun – quarrels, anger
hammer – hard work needed
hand – if open, friendship; if closed, an argument
harp – love, harmony
hat – improvement, especially a new job
hawk – jealousy
heart – pleasure, love, trust
horn – abundance
horse – if galloping, good news; if head only, a lover
horseshoe – good luck
hourglass – need to decide something
house – security
iceberg – danger
insect – problems are minor and easily overcome
jewels – gifts
kangaroo – harmony at home
kettle – any illness is minor
kite – wishes coming true
knife – broken friendship
ladder – promotion, a rise in life
lamp – at top, a feast; at side, secrets revealed; at bottom, a feast or party postponed
leaf – good fortune, new life
letter – news
lines – straight, progress; wavy, uncertain path
lion – influential friends
lock – obstacles
loop – avoid impulsive action
man – near handle, a visitor; clear and distinct, a dark person; vague, a light-coloured person
mask – excitement; insecurity
mountain – great goals but also difficulties
mouse – theft
mushroom – at top, journey or move to the country; near bottom, rapid growth, but if reversed, frustration

nail – injustice, unfairness
necklace – complete, admirers; broken, danger of losing lover
needle – recognition, admiration
oak – health, long life
octopus – danger
ostrich – travel
owl – gossip, scandal
palm tree – success, honour
parasol – new lover
parrot – a journey, but also people talking
pig – prosperity, possibly greed
pistol – danger
purse – at top, profit; at bottom, loss
question mark – need for caution
rabbit – need for bravery
rake – watch details
raven – bad news
ring – at top, marriage or an offer of marriage; at bottom, long engagement; if broken, engagement is broken off
rose – popularity
saw – interference
scale – legal issues; if balanced, a just result; if unbalanced, unjust
scissors – quarrels, possibly separation
sheep – good fortune
shell – good news
shelter – danger of loss or ill health
ship – worthwhile journey
shoe – change for the better
snake – an enemy, but also wisdom
spider – reward for work
spoon – generosity
star – health and happiness, hope
sun – happiness, success, power
sword – arguments
table – social gathering
tent – travel
thimble – changes at home
tortoise – criticism, usually beneficial
tower – disappointment
tree – improvements
triangle – something unexpected
umbrella – annoyances
urn – wealth and happiness
vase – a friend needs help
violin – egotism
volcano – harmful emotions
wagon – a wedding
wasp – romantic problems
waterfall – prosperity
wheel – if complete, good fortune; if broken, disappointment
wings – messages
wolf – jealousy
yoke – domination
zebra – adventure, especially overseas

CRYSTAL BALL GAZING

With crystal ball gazing we enter the true world of psychic divination. You do not need to see visions to read hands or interpret the Tarot. But seeing visions – clairvoyance – is exactly what happens when the practised seer looks deep into the ball of captured light.

Crystallomancy, to give it its proper name, belongs to the second sort of divination. A single image forms and the diviner interprets its meaning. With most of these methods, however, the image comes from the normal physical world. A flight of birds across the sky, the bubbles of oil in a bowl of water, the stains made by tea leaves in a clean cup – all these things lie there for anyone to see. The images in the crystal, however, arise from the clairvoyant's mind. Somehow, he or she forms a kind of partnership with the clarity of the crystal. Long practice allows him or her to clear the mind of random thought. The body relaxes and a sense of calm and patience opens within the self. The clairvoyant looks – and the image comes.

Actually, gazing does not require a crystal ball at all. Crystallomancy belongs to a wider form of divination called 'scrying', a term derived from the archaic word 'descry', meaning to see or observe. Scrying bears a long history. Chaucer, Spenser, and Shakespeare all refer to the practice. In the Bible, Joseph divined primarily from dreams but, according to tradition, he also used his cup to see future events. John Dee, the famous Renaissance alchemist and magician, gazed into a crystal ball. (Dee also served as a spy, using the code name 007, an occult number signifying willpower and victory.)

People have used all kinds of things for scrying, even their own fingernails! In Egypt and India they have gazed into blobs of ink (the famous Rorschach ink blot test could be called a form of scrying). Any smooth surface that either reflects or traps light will serve. Many people use mirrors. An old superstition tells us that a girl can descry her future husband in a mirror on Samhain, the Celtic name for New Year's Eve, now used in modern witchcraft to denote the main holiday of the year, Halloween. She need only hold the mirror up to show over her left shoulder and she will see his face. To use a mirror more systematically, blacken the back of it so it no longer reflects totally but holds the light. You can then gaze into it as you would a crystal.

Many people scry with bowls of water. The sixteenth-century French physician and astrologer Nostradamus supposedly developed his predictions by means of a combination of astrology and clairvoyance in a brass bowl filled with water. To seek such visions use a bowl with a darkened bottom. The bowl itself will then not reflect light into the water and you can use it much as you would use a crystal ball. If you do choose this method, treat the bowl with respect. Do not use it for other things and do not let other people handle it. Store it in its own place. You should also follow the methods given below for developing your scrying and clairvoyant abilities.

A deep lake on a windless day forms a giant bowl of water. Around the world people have found such a surface ideal for arousing visions. Often tradition has developed around particular bodies of water. The Greeks used a combination of mirrors and water. To find out if a sick person would recover or not they would go to a certain holy spring at Patrae. There the diviners would lower a mirror to the surface of the spring, just far enough to skim the water's surface. After saying prayers and burning incense they would raise the mirror and see the person either alive or dead. Officially this method did not depend on the ability of the seer but on the generosity of the goddess who inhabited the spring.

Despite the various methods of scrying, many people consider the crystal ball the truest and most powerful. John Melville, author of the classic text, *Crystal Gazing and Clairvoyance*, cites three kinds of image. In the first, the mind reproduces images previously observed (we could add, previously fantasized, read, or dreamt). In the second, we see things picked up from other people, either through telepathy or

Dr John Dee, the famous Elizabethan alchemist and magician. With his associate, Edward Kelly, he travelled through the English countryside in great state, practising various forms of ceremonial magic. For their sessions in clairvoyance the pair used a small, pure rock crystal and a magic scrying mirror made of natural black volcanic glass. Dr Dee recorded these visions at great length in his diaries.

Catherine de Médici with the magic mirror of Nostradamus, in which she is supposed to have seen the future of France up to the French Revolution. By the late 1550s Nostradamus was famous throughout Europe and the Queen consulted him on many occasions. The prophecies of Nostradamus are still read today.

simple conversation. We can call both the first and second categories 'visualization'. In the last, true clairvoyance, we receive genuine information. According to Melville, water or mirrors will allow the first two to take shape but only a crystal ball will show proper visions.

Crystal ball gazing in Europe goes back possibly as far as the early Christian era. We also know of crystal scrying by the Maya, Incas, and the North American Indians, as well as by the aborigines in Australia and tribal people in Borneo, and New Guinea.

The true *rock* crystal ball consists of polished beryl or quartz. Unfortunately, you probably will not find such an item very easily. Most crystal balls today are made of glass and even if you could find a rock crystal ball, it would probably cost a very great deal. People have, however, been using glass crystal balls for some time and many find them as valuable as quartz or beryl.

Crystal balls come in varying sizes. A larger ball will not ensure stronger images. Some clairvoyants will use a crystal as small as 2.5cm (1in) across. For ease of viewing, look for one at least 10cm (4in) in diameter. The interior should appear clear and luminous with as few imperfections (such as bubbles in the glass) as possible.

Once you have chosen your crystal, make sure to take proper care of it. Do not let the surface get scratched. When not using it, store the crystal ball in a safe place, covered with a soft cloth where no one will disturb it. Always keep it clean. If dirt or smudges gather on the surface, you can wash it with lukewarm water and very mild soap. Afterwards rinse it in a solution of water and alcohol or vinegar. Melville advises boiling the crystal for fifteen minutes in a solution of six parts water and one part brandy. Once you have cleaned and rinsed it, dry it with a fine linen towel and polish it with a chamois cloth.

Ideally you should keep the crystal in its own room, a small room free of mirrors, ornaments, pictures or decorations, and without any bright colours. Keep the temperature in the room at a comfortable level. Avoid letting either bright light or shadows fall on the crystal. Soft, indirect lighting will cause the least interference. The room should be free of all furniture other than the table for the crystal, a straight but comfortable chair for yourself, and one or two chairs for possible subjects. Arrange the crystal on a wooden pedestal or a soft cushion of a solid, dark colour. If necessary, arrange a dark cloth beneath the crystal to keep away reflected light. If you practise other forms of divination in addition to scrying, you might want to do these in the same room. In that case the room should contain a shelf or cabinet for storing the crystal while you are following some other method. When using the crystal you should keep the other paraphernalia out of the way. For instance, many Tarot practitioners like to frame a display of cards to hang on the wall. Such a display, however, will distract you when scrying. Cover it or move it to another room.

If, like most people, you cannot set aside a whole room for divination, try to keep a special place in the house for your crystallomancy. Choose a quiet room where you can close the door and no one will disturb you. Clear a corner of furniture, paintings, and so on and, when you sit before the crystal ball, try not to face anything that might distract you. You may wish to ask a question concerning a particular person. In that case the person may join you in the room (along with one other, no more). The person may hold the crystal ball briefly before you begin. Otherwise no one should touch the crystal but you. If other people join you, make sure they sit some distance away and do not speak or divert your attention.

Over the centuries elaborate rituals have grown up around crystal ball gazing. Most modern clairvoyants consider these practices external, stressing instead the need for a clear mind and focused patience. Still, you might want to follow some aspects of the ritual preparations, if only for the sake of tradition. One such is the building of a 'lamen', a small four-sided wooden frame to hold the crystal. The crystal sits in the centre of a square piece of wood on which the seer writes divine names. The north side receives the designation 'Tetragrammaton' (not really a name, but the English term for the Hebrew four-letter name of God Y H W H, usually transliterated as Yahweh). On the east side write 'Emmanuel', on the south 'Agla', and on the west 'Adonai'. The frame rests on a wooden pedestal which bears the name 'Saday' (a variation of 'Shaddai' which means 'Almighty'). A candlestick stands on either side of the pedestal. One displays the name 'Elohim', the other 'Elohe'. All these names derive from ceremonial magic and ultimately from Kabbala, or Jewish mysticism.

According to Meville, magicians sometimes used the crystal ball in rituals to summon demons and other spirits. Most modern diviners will avoid such practices, just as most will ignore the ancient custom of hiring a virgin boy or girl to look into the glass. A simpler tradition deals with the best time for scrying. People the world over have found that the moon enhances psychic abilities. Some scryers, therefore, try to do their seeing during periods of the moon's increase. This does not mean necessarily at night. Some diviners often prefer to work during the day, particularly at dawn or sunset. However, others will simply scry at the same time each day, regardless of the phases of the moon.

One of the elaborate rituals traditionally used in crystal ball gazing is the use of a 'lamen' or Holy Table. The ancient methods of preparation shown above are not practised widely by modern clairvoyants, except for the sake of tradition. The illustration is taken from Francis Barrett's **The Magus, or Celestial Intelligence,** *published in 1801, which played an important part in the nineteenth-century revival of ritual magic.*

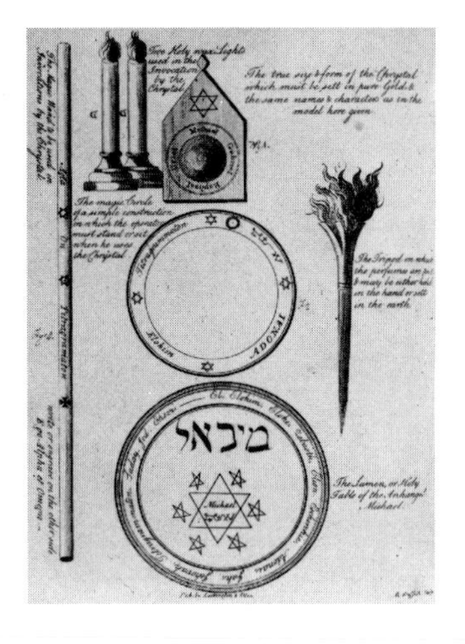

When preparing to use the crystal, spend several minutes 'charging' it. Pass the right hand over it a number of times to give it strength. Then pass the left hand over, the same number of times, for sensitivity. Repeat this for a few minutes. If nothing else, the practice will help you begin to focus your attention. After this spend a few more minutes clearing your mind. The centring exercises mentioned in the introduction become especially important here. With other forms of divination the patterns lie before you whatever you do. You then go into yourself to seek the best interpretations. In scrying the image itself depends on your ability to call it forth. Or maybe we should say, allow it to emerge. For clairvoyance – *seeing* – works best when we simply open our minds to visions.

Use your breathing. Breathe deeply and easily, taking the breath all the way in and releasing it gently. Let your breath calm you, and when you feel at rest, free of distractions, external worries and tensions, look into the crystal. Do not stare but simply keep your eyes on it. When your attention wanders (as it almost certainly will) gently bring it back.

Do not worry if you do not notice any changes the first time. Most people take quite a few sittings before they observe even the beginnings of a vision. The first day look for ten minutes only. The next time look for fifteen. After five or six sittings begin to increase your time to a maximum of one hour. If your head aches, stop for that day. If headaches persist, pay more attention to relaxation. The pain may come from muscular tension or, possibly, from the emergence of a new way of seeing, a seeing with the mind. Either way, gentle breathing and calmness can help you past the barrier.

When the crystal turns hazy or dull you are beginning to see. This stage may last several sittings or it may go away and come back. Eventually you will see clouds in the crystal. These clouds form the most common image (their interpretation is discussed below). If the crystal becomes extremely dark, wait, for it may suddenly clear and become very bright. From this brightness a sharp image may appear.

Eventually, as you become more accustomed to scrying, you will learn to focus on a particular subject and call up some relevant symbol of vision. When you begin, however, you should remain completely passive, giving the clairvoyant images

Crystal balls, together with mirrors, are the objects most commonly used for foretelling future events. Concentrated gazing upon the crystal ball will activate images from the unconscious mind.

a chance to develop in their own way.

In the tradition of crystallomancy, different clouds give different meanings. White clouds imply a 'yes' to any specific question you might have asked. More generally they form a favourable omen. Black clouds mean 'no' to a question. If they give way to brightness, this indicates a bad beginning followed by a change for the better. Violet, green, or blue clouds show coming joy. Red, orange, or yellow indicate danger or trouble. At their most ominous they may signify illness or grief. In general, however, they warn the gazer (or the subject if the gazer is looking on behalf of someone else) to prepare for an unpleasant surprise.

Ascending clouds indicate 'yes' to a question, descending 'no'. According to Melville, clouds moving to the right denote the presence of spirit beings who have taken a positive interest in the gazer. Clouds or shadows moving to the left tell the gazer that he or she should stop for now and return to the ball (or mirror or water) some other time.

Once you have accustomed yourself to scrying you can seek specific information about particular people or events. If you wish to know about a person at a certain moment, fix his or her image in your mind during your centring exercises. Similarly, you can ask about the outcome of a situation by focusing on it. In both cases, if you wish to ask about something far away (in space or time) you will need to gaze 'lengthwise' into the ball, a trick of seeing that involves shifting back a little and looking aslant. If, during your normal scrying, an image (clouds or a picture) appears far away, it implies distance (again, in space or time). If the image moves towards you, the coming event is fast approaching through changes in a situation (if it is to do with a person, he or she will soon come to you). Moving away indicates an alteration in your life which will remove the situation implied by the image.

When you begin to see specific pictures (rather than clouds or light), notice whether they appear on the right or the left. The left side shows images of actual things, the right shows symbols. For instance, a cup of champagne on the left would indicate an actual party. On the right, it would imply that there was cause for celebration. To interpret the meaning of the symbols, you can use a combination of traditional symbology and your own understanding. There are many good dictionaries of symbols. From these you will learn such traditional interpretations as 'wisdom' for a snake. However, since these particular images arise from your own unconscious, you would do well to look at what they mean to you. The images in a crystal are a little like the images in a dream. Just as most people need practice – and self-awareness – to interpret their dreams usefully, so you will need to develop skill, not just at gazing but also at understanding. Indeed, you might discover that the need to interpret benefits you more in the long run than the scrying itself.

Finally, a note of warning. As I have explained, scrying involves activating images from the unconscious. Some people consider the deep breathing and gazing into the crystal as a form of self-hypnosis. We can also compare it to the hypnagogic images people sometimes see just before falling asleep. Some of these pictures will give us true information, either as clairvoyant 'visions' or as information picked up – telepathically or subconsciously – from others. Some pictures, however, will reflect our own fantasies, desires, and fears. And others (which may include frightening images) will indicate nothing more than an eruption of the imagination (hypnagogic images often include such things as grinning beasts).

Until you learn to distinguish between the various sorts of images, take all your sightings with a certain measure of scepticism. Compare them to actual events or situations. Consider your own state of mind, especially anxieties and longings. If you can identify an image as something from your own imagination, do not dismiss it as inferior. Too many people denigrate the imagination as unimportant. Or they may go to the other extreme and take all its images literally, scaring themselves because they forget that the imagination speaks in metaphors and fantasies. Use your gazing to develop psychic skills but use it as well to learn the ways of the unconscious.

THE TAROT

FORTUNE TELLING AND THE TAROT

The Tarot is one of the great systems of divination. These systems open the user to a world far beyond that of simple fortune telling. As well as the Tarot they include the Chinese *I Ching*, the Scandinavian Runes, astrology and the Ifa divination used by the Yoruba people of Africa. All show this special double function – a method of telling fortunes that leads to spiritual wisdom.

All three belong to what I have called the first method of divination. The user takes a set of fixed pieces (a deck of cards in the case of the Tarot), each of which carries a definite meaning. He or she then mixes them up and takes several out. The pattern they form produces the reading. Since each piece has a specific interpretation, you can build important meanings into the system itself. Then, whenever you use it to answer your questions, you also expose yourself to its ideas and wisdom.

Exactly this has happened with the Tarot. Whatever its origins, it has gathered to itself over the centuries (especially the last two) a vast amount of knowledge, ideas, and even mystic experience. This process is still evolving.

You do not need to immerse yourself in philosophy or mysticism in order to appreciate or make use of the cards. Most people who have followed the Tarot's inner pathways begin with a simple desire to tell fortunes. The Tarot does not demand; it offers. Obviously, if you study texts and meditate on the symbolism, you will enter the Tarot's secrets more directly. But even if you never do any more than ask questions about relationships and job opportunities, you will still expose

Facing page: Two magnificently detailed cards from the Tarot pack long believed to have been made for the mad King Charles VI of France but which are now thought to be Italian and to date from about 1470. These early Tarot packs had no names or numbers drawn on them and the illustrations would have been clearly understood.

yourself to the Tarot's wisdom.

The Tarot contains a philosophy. It leads to an awareness of spiritual values, including optimism and the power of the soul to raise itself from despair. The Tarot provides a method of activating and understanding the imagination. It aids us in learning to confront ourselves. The way to all of these things lies through readings. At one time occult workers with the Tarot tended to denigrate the practice of readings which they regarded as trivial, even an 'insult'. Today, however, in the midst of what some people have called a 'Tarot renaissance' more and more people have come to recognize the value of readings as a practical and direct method of approaching the cards. Most serious books now being published on the Tarot will delve into such subjects as the mystic Tree of Life. They will also, however, devote a great deal of attention to readings. Here we will look at the Tarot primarily in its most common and practical context, as a method of divination.

STRUCTURE

The Tarot consists of seventy-eight cards – twenty-two trump cards, plus four suits of fourteen cards each. (The word 'trump' derives from 'triumph'; in the game of Tarot if you play a trump you will 'triumph' over opponents playing suit cards.) In occult tradition the twenty-two trumps bear the collective name Major Arcana, a term which means 'greater secrets'. The four suits together carry the name Minor Arcana, or 'lesser secrets'.

The trumps all bear names and numbers. The Fool is O, while the other cards appear in a sequence beginning with the Magician, number 1, and ending with the World, number 21. Although the very oldest decks do not carry these numbers or names they appeared fairly early on in the Tarot's history and they now belong firmly to decks used as playing cards as well as those used for fortune telling and esoteric study.

Each of the four suits bears an emblem. Older decks, and those designed in a traditional manner, show the emblems Rods (or Staves), Cups, Swords, and Coins (or Discs). Many modern decks have changed Rods to Wands and Coins to Pentacles (five-pointed stars enclosed in gold discs).

In virtually all Tarot decks the suits number 1–10, with four 'court' cards. Usually the court cards bear the names Page, Knight, Queen, and King. Each one shows the appropriate figure holding the emblem of the suit. Some modern decks have changed these designations. Following the occult Order of the Golden Dawn, occultist Aleister Crowley called his court cards Princess, Prince, Queen, and Knight. The Motherpeace Tarot (a feminist deck which is round rather than rectangular in shape) uses Daughter, Son, Shaman, and Priestess. The Native American Tarot uses Maiden, Warrior, Matriarch, and Chief.

HISTORY

No one really knows the origin of the Tarot. People have commonly associated it with the Romanies (gypsies), but the evidence indicates that this association did not begin until after the Tarot had established itself in Southern Europe. Another old theory considers the Tarot to be a coded form of ancient Egyptian magic, the 'Book of Thoth', a title which Aleister Crowley later adopted for his own Tarot deck (painted by Frieda Harris). Few students today see any real historical links with Egypt, nor do they take seriously the idea that refugees from Atlantis created the cards to encode their wisdom before it vanished for ever beneath the sea. Recently, a researcher named Barbara Walker has attempted to demonstrate that the cards derive from the goddess-worshipping Tantra tradition in India.

Aleister Crowley, the most notorious magician of the twentieth century. As well as writing his own very detailed book about the Tarot, he also designed a pack of cards which were full of erotic symbolism.

Most occultists, however, connect the Tarot primarily to Kabbala, a vast and complex system of esoteric teachings. Though Jewish in origin, the Kabbala greatly influenced magic and mysticism throughout Europe. Even today, if you read the spells in a 'grimoire' (a magician's book for calling up spirits), many of the mystical names will be derived from Hebrew. The links between Tarot and Kabbala are quite impressive. The Kabbala bases itself on the secret meanings of the twenty-two letters of the Hebrew alphabet. The Tarot, in turn, contains twenty-two trumps. The Kabbala uses the image of ten positions or 'sephiroth' on the Tree of Life. It teaches as well that there are four trees, extending through four worlds, or stages, of creation. The Tarot contains four suits, each with cards 1–10 plus four court cards. In addition, people working in this tradition have found (or created) impressive thematic connections between kabbalistic ideas and the images shown in the Tarot. One serious drawback remains in proving this theory, however. In all the thousands of pages of kabbalistic texts, with their detailed explanations and theories, no reference exists to the Tarot or anything like it. In fact, esotericists did not establish these connections until the nineteenth century, when the French occultist, Eliphas Levi, began, with others, to use the cards as a tool for working with the Kabbala. (Levi's original name was Alphonse Louis Constant. In contrast to all those European Jews who were then taking Christian names, Constant changed his name to a Hebrew one.)

The World, from the Tarot pack designed by the Italian, Bonifacio Bembo in the fifteenth century. From the Academia Carrara in Bergamo, Italy.

The lack of a historical connection with Kabbala has led many people to dismiss Levi's ideas as nonsense, along with the work of Crowley, Arthur Waite, (whose cards appear between pages 75 and 108) and the other occultists who developed this approach. Such critics might be described as throwing the baby out with the bathwater. For even if history should come down against the kabbalistic theory, the fact remains that people have made this connection, even if they have only made it in the last 150 years. We can use this knowledge, just as we can use the many new ideas and values people have found in the cards in recent years.

Still, the question of origin remains a tantalizing one. Historically, the first Tarot cards appeared in Italy around the end of the fourteenth century. In the fifteenth century the artist Bonifacio Bembo painted a number of decks for the Visconti family, rulers of Milan. One of these decks has recently been published in a mass-market edition. What did these cards mean to these people? Were they simply a game? Certainly, long before the occult revivals seized hold of the cards the *game* of '*tarocchi*' (to give it its Italian name) or '*les tarots*', as it was known in France, was played in Southern Europe. An ancestor of bridge, *les tarots* is still popular. Our ordinary playing cards probably derive from the Tarot. The cards we use for bridge or poker have simply dropped the twenty-two trumps and the four knights, reducing seventy-eight to fifty-two.

The fact that the deck has changed so little from those earlier examples implies that Bembo did not originate it but only created his own version of something already in existence. Many people believe the Tarot began as a game with images drawn

Eliphas Lévi, one of the leaders of the French occult revival in the nineteenth century. He was a prolific author and his many books on magic continue to exert a wide influence. It was Lévi who first linked the Tarot to the Kabbala.

from the ordinary life of European society, and that the occult ideas never existed in the cards which should not be taken seriously.

And yet – certain images among the trumps imply that some sort of secret meanings were hidden in the cards when they were first drawn. The card of the female pope, for example, links the Tarot to an underground tradition of resistance to an all-male clergy. In the year 1300 the Church burned to death a woman named Manfreda Visconti. A sect known as the Guglielmites had chosen Manfreda as the first female pope in a supposedly new age in which women would occupy the papacy. Pope Manfreda belonged to the same Visconti family for whom Bembo painted his cards nearly one and a half centuries later.

And what must we make of the Hanged Man? The illustration on page 79 shows a man hanging upside down, an ancient image of spiritual awakening. In yoga people stand on their heads to help move the energy from the base of the spine to the brain. In the Runes chapter we will see that the god Odin hung on a tree for nine days in order to receive the secret wisdom.

In the nineteenth century Eliphas Levi began his great linking of Tarot and Kabbala. Esoteric decks began to appear, some with Hebrew letters on the card (a practice still found on many decks today). Around the turn of the century Levi's ideas began to spread abroad, especially to England where occult groups began using the Tarot in their rituals. The most famous of these was the Order of the Golden Dawn (mentioned above) which developed its own Tarot deck, changing some of the numbers and images.

The last few years have seen a great resurgence of interest in the Tarot with literally hundreds of new decks being produced. Many of their designers have re-created the ancient images and linked them to various traditions varying from Tibetan Buddhism, the *I Ching,* and Tantra, to initiation practices among the Maya. Quite a number of 'women's Tarots' have appeared, utilizing goddess images from around the world in place of the normal designs. People have created Tarots specifically to aid meditation or healing. Others have linked the cards to cultural traditions, such as the Native American Tarot with its scenes from the Indian cultures of North and South America.

A number of serious artists have also painted decks. Salvador

Dali's paintings and collages combine images taken from art history and the work of famous artists, with the occult symbolism of the Tarot tradition. In Italy, home of the oldest decks, a number of young artists have produced cards as works of contemporary art. Also in Italy the sculptress Niki de Saint Phalle has created a massive 'Tarot pack' from concrete with some of the trump figures as large as buildings.

THE RIDER PACK

The cards shown between pages 75 and 108 are called the 'Rider pack' after their original publishers, the Rider Company of London. Designed by Arthur Edward Waite and painted by Pamela Colman Smith, they first appeared in 1910. They have since proved the most popular Tarot, appearing in various editions. Many recent decks have based their designs, particularly in the suit cards, on Pamela Smith's scenes and images. You will notice that the Rider pack uses roman numerals. I prefer to use Arabic numerals as these have more significance in readings.

Waite made certain changes in the trumps, altering the Lovers, Death, the Emperor, and the Sun. Following the Golden Dawn he switched around Strength and Justice. Traditionally Strength is 11 and Justice 8. In the Rider pack they show up respectively as 8 and 11. Though Waite considered these changes important, the deck's popularity stems much more from the Minor Arcana. In all previous decks the numbered cards had simply displayed a formal design. For instance, the 4 of Swords would show four crossed swords against a plain background. The 8 of Cups might show eight cups arranged in rows. For the Rider pack, however, Pamela Smith drew an actual scene on every card. In the 4 of Swords a knight lies on a stone table in a church. Swords hang above and below him. In the 8 of Cups a man climbs a hill under the full moon. At the bottom stand eight cups.

The use of the Rider pack here does not mean that readers must use this particular set of cards. A wide variety of Tarot decks is now on sale. Choose the one which most appeals to you. You may find that you prefer one of the older decks. Many people like the sense of tradition these provide. Or you might find yourself drawn to one of the more recent decks. Many of

Arthur Edward Waite, photographed by E.O. Hoppé. He was an American who spent most of his life in England and became a member of the Order of the Golden Dawn. Together with Pamela Colman Smith, he designed the best-known modern Tarot pack and he wrote the standard English introduction to the Tarot.

these follow the Rider pack by depicting a scene on each card, and the artist has frequently based his or her choices largely on Smith's drawings. The meanings will also remain very close.

You might find yourself drawn to more than one deck. Many people who become involved with the Tarot end up as collectors. An acquaintance of mine owns an entire bookcase filled with cards, from antique ones, which are centuries old, to new cartoon cards, created as publicity material for a James Bond film. It is not uncommon to own between ten and twenty sets of cards. Some people continue to use one special deck out of their collection, while others use several. One friend of mine uses different decks for readings, depending on the person and the kind of question she wants to ask.

Two cards from the 007 Tarot pack designed by Fergus Hall for the James Bond film, **Live and Let Die.**

You will probably want to begin with one deck. Learn it well and develop a relationship with it. When you first bring it home, spend some time with the pictures before you begin readings. Explore your own reactions to the cards. Whatever deck you buy will probably come with an instruction booklet. This will give brief meanings for each of the cards. Read the descriptions and then compare these to the cards themselves. Choose cards at random; lay them next to each other and let them stimulate your imagination. The Italian novelist, Italo Calvino, once called the Tarot 'a machine for telling stories'. See what stories your cards produce when you place them beside each other or move them around.

If you choose a deck other than the Rider pack you can still use the meanings given here since they will work with any set of cards. You can also work with the meanings given in the instruction booklet in conjunction with those given here. As you become more practised, you will develop a sense of what your cards mean to *you*. If an entirely new interpretation of a particular card suggests itself to you, either in a specific reading or in general, do add it to your set of possible meanings.

Most people who work with Tarot cards keep them in a wooden box or wrapped in silk. You should also not let people handle your cards, except when mixing them for a reading. Keep them in a special place when not working with them. Do not treat your cards frivolously. If you wish to play the game of *les tarots,* you should use a separate deck, preferably one of those designed as playing cards.

THE MAJOR ARCANA

Each of the trump cards carries its own meanings for use in readings. To understand these meanings fully, however, we should look briefly at the ideas developed by the Major Arcana as a group.

There are two ways of viewing the Major Arcana. In readings we draw upon both of these to understand what specific cards mean to us. The first approach sees the trumps as a collection of qualities and attitudes valuable for living. In this sense the Magician represents creativity, positive action, and a sense of personal power. The High Priestess signifies peacefulness and a sense of mystery. Other cards teach lessons we need to learn to get along in life. For instance, the Wheel of Fortune shows us that things always change and that we should not consider any condition permanent. Death teaches us that all things must end and give way to others.

The second approach considers the trumps as a sequence. Beginning with the Magician and the High Priestess, the cards continue, step by step, until the World. Looked at in this way the meaning of Temperance, for example, depends not only on the image but also on the card's place as number 14, coming after 1–13, and before 15, the Devil.

There are many interpretations of this sequence. Some are highly specific, such as the kabbalistic links to the twenty-two pathways on the Tree of Life. A more general view sees the Major Arcana as a description of the soul's journey through life. The Fool represents the soul itself. As 0 it exists before birth. It enters the world which is governed by the two basic principles of life, the Magician and the High Priestess, symbolizing light and dark, positive and negative, male and female. After these two abstractions the Empress and the Emperor signify the child's parents. The Hierophant is its education, the Lovers its sexual awakening, and so on. As the culminating card, the World denotes the soul which has achieved its goals in life. Many people then move the Fool to the end, to illustrate the concept of reincarnation. The soul then begins its round once more in a new body.

A similar, though more specific approach treats the Major Arcana as the progress of a seeker on the path to enlightenment.

Once again, the Fool represents the person travelling through the different stages of the trumps. Again the Magician and the High Priestess signify the two poles of existence. But this time they carry more precise meanings. The Magician is the adept, the master of knowledge and power. The High Priestess sits before a veil, for the card represents the mysteries to which the initiate will be privy.

How do such esoteric interpretations affect ordinary people? Does the Major Arcana matter only in the rarefied rituals of occultists? Many people consider the occult a land of strange doctrines and stranger practices, whose inhabitants seek magical powers. Such goals and methods do exist. At its best, however, the occult tradition seeks something more fundamental – to overcome the weaknesses, ignorance, confusion, and misery of life, in short, to become a whole person. The aim is not just to know mysterious secrets but to know oneself and the truth of the world.

Since the Tarot deals with such fundamental questions as love, striving for success, and the necessity for change, its images apply to us all, whether we follow an esoteric path or not. In our readings we may not think consciously of the mysteries represented by the Major Arcana. None the less those mysteries will still influence what the cards mean to us and it is through them that the Major Arcana helps us to understand the daily situations we encounter in life.

Most people who interpret the Major Arcana as a sequence divide it up in some way. Some see it as two halves with the break coming at the Wheel of Fortune. The first half deals with the outer concerns of life, such as career, marriage, and the achievement of success and power. At a certain point we will realize the limitations of such things and turn inward on a quest for self-knowledge, represented by the second half.

Others, myself included, divide the Major Arcana into three rows of seven, arranged in numerical order, together with the Fool (see Figure 24). As the only card without an ordinary number, the Fool belongs both everywhere and nowhere. He represents the seeker. The first row of seven cards shows the person encountering the basic challenges of life such as parents, education, sexual awakening, and success. It culminates in the Chariot, a card of triumph. But then, with Strength and the

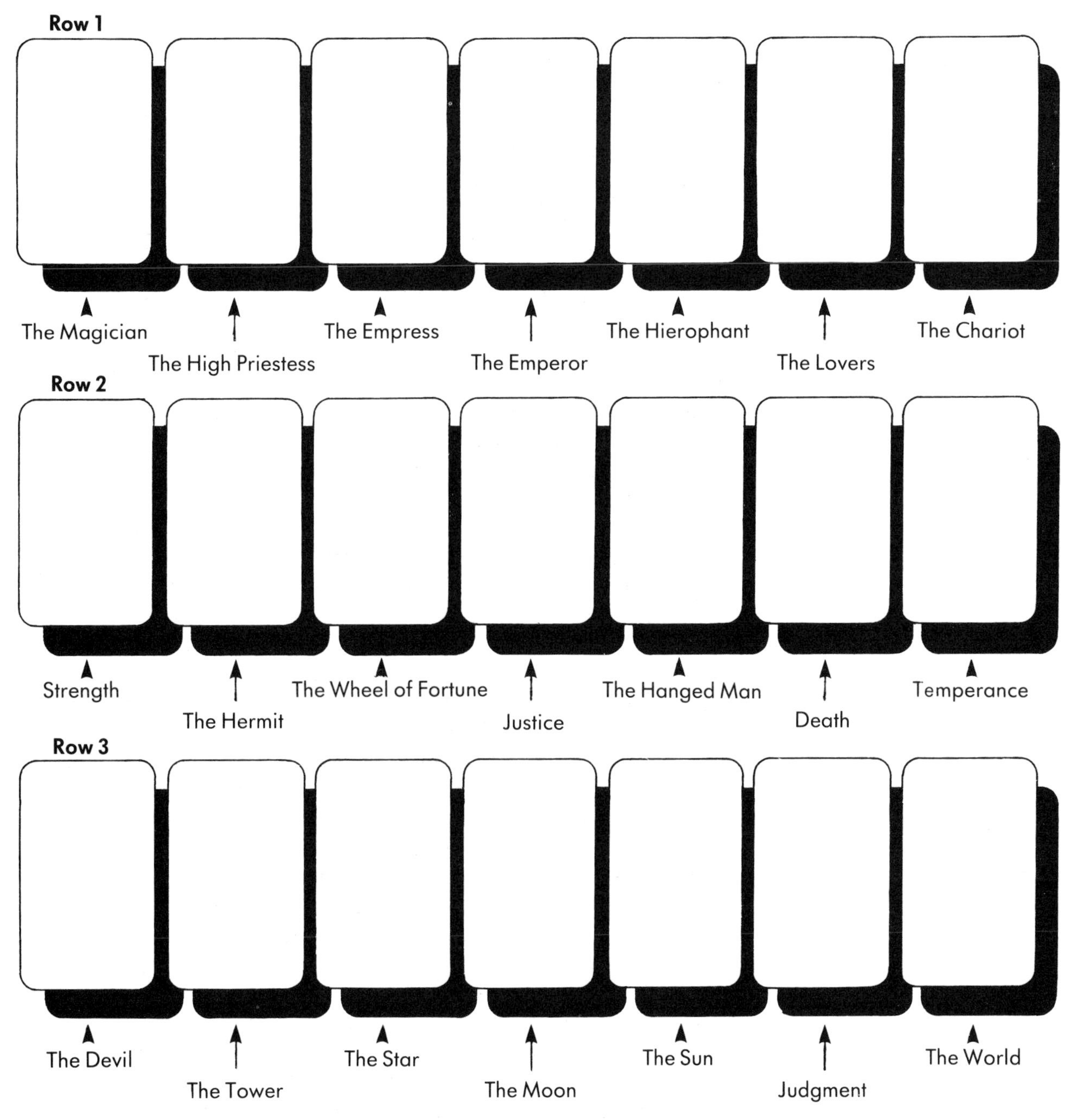

Figure 24. The Major Arcana divided into three rows of seven cards

Hermit, the person turns away from outward victories. He or she recognizes the need to understand the self (the Wheel of Fortune, and Justice), becomes aware of fundamental values instead of simply conforming to social conventions (the Hanged Man), and is therefore able to let go of rigidities and outworn habits (Death). It ends with the inner triumph of Temperance.

If the first row of seven cards deal with outer success and the second with inner awareness, what remains for the final seven? We live in a time which looks primarily at the self. For many people psychology has replaced religion in life and psychology deals with personal issues. The Tarot reminds us of concerns outside ourselves. The last seven cards then deal with universal forces. They take up such questions as the truth within the unconscious, the distortions of fear and the imagination, and the bringing together of opposites. The most powerful of the trumps, they work in readings to tell us much about our ordinary lives.

The Fool: Without a fixed place the Fool moves through the cards, giving us the courage to continue. When we think we have found somewhere we can stop, the Fool prods us to move on and seek new experience. Symbolizing the instinct for life, the Fool dances lightly on the edge of the cliff, ready to jump into the unknown. He reminds us not to cling to what we have but to give it up and take the leap. The number 0 means that he is indefinable, refusing to link himself with possessions or achievements, ideas or public recognition. He is nothing and therefore everything.

In a reading the Fool urges the individual to trust his or her instincts, even if these appear to lead in a foolish direction. The Fool advises the subject to take chances rather than play safe. When faced with a choice of security or the unknown, the Fool always recommends the latter. The person should follow his or her own instinct rather than the advice of others. This last meaning becomes especially strong when the Fool appears with the Hanged Man.

Reversed (upside down), the Fool indicates someone cut off from his or her instincts. It can signify fear of taking a chance but also wild behaviour. Either way, the person needs to recognize what he or she really wants from the situation.

Row One of the Major Arcana, and the Fool

The Magician: The Magician stands for creative power and the 'masculine' principle of action. Esoteric tradition looks at the world as the mixing of two poles, calling them positive and negative, light and dark, active and passive, male and female. In the Tarot we see the male and female as the Magician and the High Priestess. This does not mean that the Magician can apply only to a man. Each of us mixes masculine and feminine qualities and at one time or another we will experience one side more strongly than the other. The Magician represents the experience of power and of making things happen in your life. It is important to do something with this power, to convert it into actions and the achievement of goals. The Magician can easily influence others with his magnetic personality. His real purpose, however, is to 'make the flowers grow'. In questions about specific projects, the Magician indicates the ability, and usually the will, to succeed.

The High Priestess: We often think of active as good and passive as bad. In fact, we need the High Priestess as much as we do the Magician. She represents those times when it is better to sit still rather than attempt grand enterprises. She signifies mystery and intuition, the secrets of life and of ourselves, which we know unconsciously but cannot put into words. We come to such awareness only through stillness.

The High Priestess denotes a time when the person should do nothing active but rather seek peace within the self. Instead of involving herself with other people she keeps 'silent'. The veil behind the High Priestess and her rolled-up scroll signify mysteries, either actual secrets or things sensed but not understood.

Reversed, the High Priestess indicates a return to passion. The person will become involved with other people, with projects and excitement. He or she must take care that these actions come naturally and not from a fear of being alone.

The Empress: The High Priestess represents half of what we call the 'female archetype' – the stillness and silent mystery of life. The Empress signifies the other side – that of passion and sensual involvement with the world. She is at once lover and mother, for both give themselves totally. For a woman or a man the Empress indicates a time of passion, of sexual desire and enjoyment of life. Depending on the other cards this can lead either to benefits or problems, for the Empress can signify self-indulgence. Sometimes the Empress may stand for the person's mother, and her influence in his or her life. Alternatively, it can refer to the subject showing a motherly concern for someone else.

Reversed, the Empress indicates that the person turns away from passion. Usually this denotes analysis rather than repression, the careful working out of some complicated problem through thought rather than emotion.

The Emperor: Where the Empress signifies passion, the Emperor represents structure and control. He symbolizes authority, law, and rules. Although these things are often necessary, they can become repressive. Notice that no flowers grow around him and that the river (the water of life) has narrowed to a stream cutting its way through the rock.

The Emperor often signifies someone very powerful in the person's life, sometimes a father or a husband. Whoever he is, he *rules* and the subject feels under his influence.

Reversed, the Emperor becomes compassionate and more emotional although this can degenerate into sloppy or uncontrolled behaviour.

There is a deeper side to the Emperor too. He can symbolize not just the laws of society but the laws of life. If the person cannot stand being bound by rules and if this is a source of unhappiness, perhaps making relationships impossible, then he or she may need to explore the inner truth of the Emperor.

The Hierophant: Traditionally the Hierophant (also called the Pope) represents organized religion. For some he may symbolize secret teachings. Either way, he denotes a path laid out for his disciples. In a reading the Hierophant indicates conformity and doing what is socially expected. He may, therefore, symbolize social institutions, particularly marriage or some other kind of formal relationship. Whether this relationship contains inner meaning or continues only as a formality depends on the other cards. For instance, the Lovers or the 2 of Cups would imply that it was based on love. The Lovers reversed would suggest that the passion had gone out of the marriage.

Reversed, the Hierophant indicates unorthodoxy and a nonconformist. This is often admirable but it can lead to gullibility, the person taking up whatever new idea comes along.

The Lovers: Older versions of this card showed a young man having to choose between two women. It often, therefore, indicated a difficult choice. In a wider sense it symbolized the problems of sexuality. The Rider pack version of the Lovers, however, represents the power of a mature sexual union. The two people are naked, open to each other. The angel above them stands for the truth and strength found in their relationship, something neither could have achieved alone. In a reading the card shows an important and usually long-lasting relationship. If the person is unattached the Lovers may point to a future relationship. If the reading concerns something unrelated to sex or love, the Lovers may signify help from a lover.

Reversed, the Lovers indicates problems in a relationship, an estrangement or quarrelsome period. Alternatively, it can also suggest sexual immaturity.

The Chariot: Traditionally this card bears the surname 'victory'. As the final card in the first line of seven, it indicates someone who is victorious over the external problems of life, in other words someone successful and established with a powerful and confident personality. The Charioteer approaches life (or a specific situation) through willpower. He or she triumphs through determination. We should not underestimate the value of this quality. We can sometimes find the will to go forward by mentally focusing on the image of the Chariot. And yet, the trump remains limited. Force of personality alone cannot dominate every situation. Some things require surrender.

Reversed, the Chariot signifies weakness and it may show a lack of will to continue when faced with a difficult problem. In extreme cases, where the person has tried to hold his or her life together by willpower, it can suggest that the contradictions are pulling the person apart. In other circumstances, however, it may reveal a new approach, free of the need to dominate.

Strength: The second row of cards looks inward to a confrontation with the self. As the first card, Strength brings us the qualities necessary for this task: openness instead of determination, quiet confidence instead of dominance. Strength means the inner strength to accept yourself. The Chariot represents a masculine power. Our society tends to forget that gentleness can hold a greater strength and this card shows the person facing problems with confidence and hope.

The lion on the card symbolizes the passions: anger as well as desire. Instead of repressing or controlling them, the woman allows them to emerge. She tames the lion through love and through belief in herself. In a reading this imagery shows that the person can allow 'negative' feelings to come out in a positive context. It tells us not to fear our emotions.

Reversed, Strength indicates weakness and pessimism. It can also suggest someone troubled by complex emotions and afraid to face them. Sometimes Strength may reveal a desire for weakness, as an excuse for giving up.

The Hermit: The Hermit withdraws from the world in order to find wisdom. Hermits will literally travel to deserts or the tops of mountains in order to escape the distractions of society.

Row Two of the Major Arcana

Isolation allows the mind to look inwards. Of course, few people will take such drastic steps just because they receive the Hermit in a Tarot reading. None the less the card does call for a shift of attention, away from other people, from amusements or plans, and towards an examination of yourself and your life.

In contrast to the disciples who kneel before the Hierophant, the Hermit finds his own way up the mountain and, therefore, indicates seeking solutions on your own. He appears as an old man, thus representing maturity.

A teacher, the Hermit does not seek wisdom only for himself. At times in readings the card denotes someone who will give guidance or help.

Reversed, the Hermit brings several possibilities. It can signify a fear of being alone or an over-dependence on others. Sometimes it shows a Peter Pan complex – the refusal to grow up. At other times, however, it tells the subject that this is not the time to withdraw from others. The interpretation will depend on the other cards.

Wheel of Fortune: The tenth trump represents the Tarot's image of fate, or karma. As the wheel turns, life changes. We can never count on things staying the same. The appearance of this card in a reading tells the person that events will turn round in some fashion, the situation will change of its own accord, through actions or circumstances beyond his or her control. According to some traditional interpretations, right side up shows a downfall, while reversed it indicates the person's fortunes rising. Psychologically it might make more sense to interpret right side up as the ability to adapt to the new situation. Reversed would then indicate the person trying to fight against the changes.

Justice: As the eleventh trump, Justice stands at the midpoint of the twenty-two trumps. It involves an examination of the person's life, or more immediately, of the situation described in the readings. It calls on the subject to weigh everything carefully (notice the balanced scales), to accept responsibility for what he or she has done and to understand what the other people in the situation have done. The scales also balance past and future. The upright sword symbolizes the keen mind, able to cut through illusions and to pick out the facts. This card tells the person to analyse the situation and differentiate between one thing and another. This does not mean that things should be approached without feeling. The picture combines imagery from both the Magician and the High Priestess and this tells us that an instinctive honesty lies behind rational examination.

Reversed, Justice indicates someone who is denying responsibility. 'It's unfair,' reversed Justice says, or, melodramatically, 'It's all my fault.' Either way, it avoids a real examination of the situation. In a legal context Justice (or Justice reversed) denotes a fair (or unfair) result.

The Hanged Man: One of the Tarot's strongest and most powerful images, the Hanged Man shows us someone connected to the deep currents of life. All over the world people recognize the symbol of the World Tree which grows from the underworld to heaven, from past to future, from the unconscious mysteries to the highest spiritual awareness. By attaching himself to the tree, that is to life, the Hanged Man frees himself from fears and the pressures of society. In readings, therefore, he shows someone who knows his or her own mind, someone independent with his or her own values. As it comes after

Justice, the Hanged Man's peace and self-reliance often follow a difficult period, especially one of self-examination.

Reversed, the Hanged Man indicates someone overly worried about other people's opinions. He or she may avoid doing something because of what people might say. It tells us that we need to find our own values, our own sense of who we are and what matters to us.

Death: This card does not represent physical death. Instead, it signifies the dying away of old habits, old fears (or hopes), old relationships, and old ways of dealing with the world. If we oppose change – like the old king lying on the ground – then the experience of Death can seem shattering. If we welcome change, however, – like the child kneeling with flowers – then we will find that Death leads to new life and new possibilities.

In readings Death signifies something the person needs to give up. It can refer to something very specific, or, alternatively, to a whole approach to life. The person may find this release very difficult or painful. We do not give up habits easily, especially if they've helped us in the past. And to give up some long-held hope – or even a fear – means facing the future without any fixed idea of what is going to happen. But the time has come for something new and only Death can make room for it.

Reversed, Death indicates a fear of change and an attempt to hang on to the old ways. It sometimes appears as the key card in a difficult reading.

Temperance: The fourteenth trump ends the second line with a vision of the new life that comes after Death. We see a powerful being pouring water from one cup to another. This pouring symbolizes the ability to combine different elements in life, such as work and pleasure, love and sex, feeling and action, openness and confidence. The image of one foot in water and one on land denotes a similar blending (water represents emotions, land represents action). Where the Chariot showed victory over the outside world, Temperance indicates victory over doubts and rigidities.

In a reading Temperance advises a cautious attitude. It stands for moderation and taking the middle way, never going to one extreme or the other. It suggests compromise instead of battle.

Many people find Temperance boring. Some workers with Tarot prefer the Devil with its excesses. But these people see only the outward form of Temperance, the caution and holding back. Within, Temperance means autonomy and having control over your own life.

Reversed, Temperance indicates that the person has lost the middle way. In a tense situation this can be dangerous and weaken the person emotionally. It is a reminder to calm down.

The Devil: The third line is a line of challenges and powerful forces. The Devil signifies the challenge of repression and of illusions. The people in the picture appear trapped, chained to the Devil's stone. In fact, the loops are wide enough for them to lift off the chains and walk away. What traps them is the belief that they can do nothing. Notice their relaxed poses. They have simply accepted their condition and are not struggling against imprisonment. Notice too that the Devil has transformed them into demons. In exchange for their safe situation they have given up part of their humanity.

The Devil signifies an oppressive situation that is controlling the subject. It can refer to a particular person with power over him or her, or just to the situation itself. Most important, it implies the illusion of helplessness. In this deck the Devil appears as a parody of the Lovers. (The Devil is 15, and 1 + 5 = 6, the Lovers.) Though the Devil can refer to many things (economic problems, for instance) it most often represents sexual relationships that have become obsessive and destructive.

Reversed, the Devil shows the subject seeking to free him or herself from the Devil's power. This attempt may give rise to feelings of depression, repressed anger or fear, especially if he or she has accepted the Devil for a long time. The reading can help the person continue the struggle.

The Tower: Accepting the Devil may seem easier than fighting it but, in fact, it creates internal pressure which will eventually lead to an explosion or crisis. The Tower represents some sort of upheaval in life. At the time the person may experience it as destructive, even violent. And yet, the bolt of lightning clears away the stone tower that imprisons us, keeping us from exploring our lives.

Row Three of the Major Arcana

If we set the Major Arcana in lines of seven then the Tower comes two rows below the High Priestess. In its deepest sense it shows the lightning bolt of truth. Therefore, in a reading it can signify some shocking revelation. More commonly, the connection reminds us that the upheaval releases the pent-up emotions. Like Death, the Tower brings liberation but, as with Death, the person may find it a very difficult experience.

Reversed, the Tower indicates that the person tries to contain the explosion. While it becomes less powerful, it also becomes less liberating. The old problems may remain, relieved of only some of the pressures.

The Star: One of the Tarot's loveliest images, the Star embodies the peace and confidence that come after the explosions of the Tower. The card signifies hope, calm, and a relaxed but eager frame of mind. The woman's nakedness symbolizes openness and confidence. Unlike most of the trump figures, she does not stand or sit in a fixed pose but kneels freely and at ease, halfway between action and stillness. Like Temperance she keeps one foot on land, one on water. The Star's freedom goes beyond moderation, however. She pours out her water without any need to conserve her energy or keep herself under control. Her calm confidence in life carries her through all situations.

Reversed, the Star indicates that the person has closed off hope and confidence. He or she fears to take such an open, relaxed attitude. This fear may result in tiredness or depression. The person does not have to accept this condition, however, since the presence of the Star at all implies the possibility of its great benefits. It simply becomes a matter of recognizing that possibility.

The Moon: The Moon belongs to the realm of the imagination, fantasies, and dreams. Its reflected light has always aroused strange passions. In this trump alone no humans appear. The lunar power has changed them to a dog and a wolf. In other words, the Moon brings out the animal, the primeval side in us. The crayfish symbolizes the very deep fears we can never name, for they come from within ourselves. It crawls halfway from its deep pool (the unconscious). Such fears never entirely surface but will always sink back again. If we accept this strange side of ourselves then the Moon will calm as well as arouse.

In readings the Moon signifies fears and anxieties but also fantasies, even psychic talent.

Reversed, the Moon indicates that the person feels uncomfortable with this side of him or herself. Fighting or suppressing it often increases its power, especially the power to disturb.

The Sun: A much simpler card than the Moon, the Sun represents joy, freedom, and a sense of rebirth and simplicity. Most older versions of this card showed a boy and girl standing together in a garden. That image implied a resolution of the opposing forces that appeared earlier in the trumps. By depicting a single child riding out of a garden the Rider pack emphasizes optimism, excitement, and fresh opportunities. Under the Sun's direct light all the fears and mysteries vanish. Everything becomes simple with this card, at times too simple. Still, we should enjoy the Sun whenever we can.

Reversed, the Sun's benefits do not vanish, though it does lose some of that simplicity. We can describe it symbolically as a cloud passing over the sun.

Judgment: This trump depicts a resurrection. We see a man and a woman with a child between them. The child symbolizes a new life after the person has faced all the challenges. We call it 'Judgment' because, like Justice, it requires coming to terms with yourself, going down to rise up. When we lay the cards out in lines of seven, Judgment comes directly below Death.

In readings Judgment can signify a special moment in life. Whatever goes on outside the person, something is pushing from within, calling him or her to change their life in an important way. Like the angel Gabriel summoning the dead souls, the call urges the person to rise up and seek new possibilities.

Reversed, Judgment indicates the person fighting against the changes. The call still sounds from within but he or she tries to ignore it by hanging on to the old life with its safe patterns. The subject may think of objections that make change impossible. However rational these appear, they are really excuses.

The World: The culminating card of the Major Arcana gives us an image of wholeness and freedom. Though we see her as a woman, tradition describes her as a hermaphrodite, combining the (symbolic) qualities of male and female. The magic wand represents the Magician but she carries two of them, denoting the High Priestess. And she dances. Of all the trumps, only the Fool and the World dance. They are not archetypes of one kind, or stage, of experience. They are complete beings. But where the Fool's completeness depended on his innocence, the World transforms innocence to wisdom. She knows about life and about pain. And yet she will dance for joy.

In readings the World indicates the ability to overcome problems, obstacles, and sorrow. With specific questions it denotes success and achievement.

Reversed, the World represents stagnation, life stopped at a certain point. Difficulties may block the person or he or she may fear to reach for the possibilities implied by the card.

THE MINOR ARCANA

The Minor Arcana consists of four suits: Wands, Cups, Swords, and Pentacles. In older decks and in many modern ones the last suit is often called Coins or Discs. Each suit has fourteen cards: Ace through 10, plus Page, Knight, Queen, and King. Many historians believe that modern playing cards developed from the Tarot suits with Wands becoming clubs, Cups hearts, Swords spades, and Coins diamonds. Along the way the Knight dropped out and the Page became a knave or jack. Of the trumps, only the Fool remained, transformed into the joker (who, like the Fool, belongs everywhere).

If the Major Arcana has evolved over the centuries into a description of the soul's progress, the modern Minor Arcana forms an encyclopedia of ordinary experience. This is especially true of the Rider pack. Pamela Smith's drawings on the numbered cards depict such scenes as a successful man bored with life, the beginning and end of love affairs, a man lost in daydreams of glory and adventure, and a woman nostalgic for the lost security of childhood.

The scenes do not form a random collection. The four suits structure themselves around the concept of the four elements: Earth, Air, Fire, and Water. In medieval Europe (and in many other cultures, from the ancient Chinese to the Navaho Indians) people believed that all existence was built up from combinations of basic elements. Today we recognize them as highly complex mixtures of compounds and processes which, in fact, include some ninety natural elements, such as oxygen, iron, and uranium. The old elements, however, differed from the modern ones in a very important way since they also described aspects of experience and human behaviour. We still speak of people as 'fiery' or 'earthy'. In the Tarot the qualities of each element help determine the kind of scenes we see in the different suits.

Wands belong to the element of Fire. The Wands cards, therefore, show scenes of action, excitement, adventure, and optimism, all the qualities we associate with Fire and fiery personalities. Fire lacks direction, however, and Wands' energy is sometimes undisciplined, without a clear goal or plan. Fire conquers and Wands cards can depict success and achievement. Yet Fire needs freedom, and success can sometimes impose a sense of confinement, as is shown in the King, the 10, or the 2.

Cups belong to Water, which flows rather than forces, giving way rather than resisting. Cups cards show scenes of love and gentleness. As water symbolizes the unconscious (which is mysterious, with hidden depths), and since it can take any shape, Cups stand for fantasy and inspiration. Water lacks the power of Fire, however, and it can become passive, too bound up in itself, and unable to take direct action.

Swords are the most complex of the four suits. As Air, they symbolize mental activity, for the mind is like the wind, swift and constantly changing direction. Swords cards show sorrow and pain but also analysis and truth. The Ace depicts an upright sword of truth piercing through the crown of illusion. As weapons Swords also symbolize conflict and aggression (Air creating storms). They can signify the pains and defeats life inflicts on us, and for this reason many people find them frightening in a reading. We must keep things in perspective and remember that these form only one part of our lives.

Pentacles derive from the element Earth. Where the other suits symbolize states of mind or types of experience, Pentacles refer to the outside world. They are concerned with money, nature, work, and prosperity. The opposite of Wands, Pentacles prefer society to adventure, discipline and hard work to freedom. Though some of the cards in this suit tend toward stodginess and work for work's sake, they also indicate the satisfaction to be gained from creating something very real in your world. As magic signs, Pentacles symbolize the magic hidden within nature and ordinary life.

Though we will look at each suit on its own, the four elements also balance each other, especially in readings. As phallic symbols, Wands and Swords represent 'masculine' or forceful qualities. Cups and Pentacles form the 'feminine', or receptive, half of the Minor Arcana. On the other hand, Wands and Cups tend to show more positive experiences, while Swords and Pentacles denote the more difficult aspects of life. Finally, Wands and Pentacles deal with practical concerns, while Cups and Swords depict the emotions.

WANDS

King: Kings show the suit in its most powerful form. The King denotes someone strong, with a powerful belief in himself and his achievements. He sits firmly on his throne, able to dominate others through willpower and self-confidence. He sometimes tends toward arrogance, especially with people less successful and less sure of themselves. The King also represents responsibility. He has channelled his Fire to developing a career, personal achievement, and his family. This goes somewhat against his Fire nature, however, so we see a certain impatience since he would prefer to leave all the attendant responsibilities to someone else while he goes off to seek adventure. He may long for the days when he rode free as a knight.

Reversed, the Wands court cards show the effect of obstacles and hardship on all that Fire optimism. The King stays powerful but he develops both sympathy and tolerance for those weaker than himself.

Queen: The Queens indicate an appreciation of the suit's basic quality. The Queen of Wands, therefore, shows a love of life and an eagerness for experience. She is wise, passionate, and an optimist. Alone among the Queens, she sits with her legs apart, a sign of a strong sexual appetite. The black cat (a witch's 'familiar' or spirit in attendance) sits like a guardian at her feet. The Queen approaches life with such openness and faith that the world seems to take care of her. Like the King, she is honest and sincere, but in contrast to him, she does not dominate others.

Reversed, the Queen indicates that, faced with trouble, her good nature tries to solve things. She is positive and cheerful but may turn bitter, nasty, or unfaithful unless the problems are resolved. Life, to her, means joy and she might find it hard to cope with too much sorrow.

Knight: Knights are younger (in spirit if not in age) than Kings or Queens and less established in life. For the Knight of Wands this means freedom, adventure, movement, and travel. In readings, the Knight of Wands may, therefore, indicate a journey. The Knight approaches situations with eagerness and self-confidence, sometimes more than is justified. For he does not always know where he is going and, without concrete plans, may burn out before he can achieve his goals.

Reversed, the card shows that the untried Knight charges into battle with more courage than skill. Real opposition – from a person or from a situation – can knock him off his horse. The reversed Knight may symbolize confusion, interruption, or delays.

Facing page: The suit of Wands

KING of WANDS
QUEEN of WANDS.
KNIGHT of WANDS.
PAGE of WANDS.
X
IX
VIII
VII
VI
V
IV
III
II
ACE of WANDS.

Page: In any reading the court cards may refer to some aspect of the subject of the reading or to a specific person influencing the subject. Pages are children but they can also symbolize a childlike openness. Less active than the Knights, they are also less forceful. Pages represent beginnings; as, indeed, does the suit of Wands. The Page of Wands, therefore, indicates the beginning of something, whether this is a project, a love affair, or simply a new phase in someone's life. Alternatively, he may represent a firm decision about a question. Romantically, he symbolizes a faithful lover.

Reversed, the card indicates that problems leave the Page confused. He finds it hard to decide about anything. Since he dislikes complexity, if he cannot see a simple solution to a problem he may become weak. Romantically he represents unfaithfulness.

10: This card denotes someone burdened by life. Like the businessman in the 'rat race', his responsibilities wear him down. Very often he or she has actually willingly taken on these burdens. Initially these may have begun as exciting projects and challenges, stimulating work, or pleasurable romantic involvements. Success means that the person cannot let go of them or delegate. He has lost his freedom. In relationships this card indicates someone who takes all the responsibility for keeping the relationship alive. By trying to smooth everything over, however, resentments are stifled.

Reversed, two meanings are possible. Either the burdens increase until the person can no longer carry them; alternatively, he or she has cast them off. This can mean rejecting responsibility by walking out of a situation. It can also show a more open and mature approach to problems and a recognition that a problem shared is a problem halved.

9: This card shows a Wands way of confronting difficulties. We see a strong man, able to defend himself. He is bandaged but still alert. But he is also stubborn, his only stance being one of defensiveness or aggression. He has become so used to adopting this attitude that he may get into situations from which it is difficult to extricate himself. Notice the raised shoulder and the bandage around the head. In a relationship he or she may continue to fight, even when the other person wants to surrender.

Reversed, a 9 may represent a less defensive approach or, that the defences are in danger of failing. The other cards will help determine the best interpretation.

8: This card shows eight wands flying through the air towards the ground which conveys the idea of matters reaching a conclusion, of action with a definite end in view. It can mean the end of a long journey or that a project of some duration is concluded. As a card of advice rather than prediction, it tells the person to avoid aimless activity. Actions with specific goals should be undertaken rather than vague or long-term projects.

When applied to romantic situations the card shows what Waite calls 'the arrows of love', and it can indicate a new relationship.

Reversed, the image depicts a situation that either continues indefinitely or does not lead to clear results. Romantically it denotes the arrows of jealousy.

7: One aspect of life revealed by the suit of Wands is the excitement of conflict. The 9 shows someone who has become defensive and weary but the 7 indicates the way in which a strong person can find battle exhilarating, as long, that is, as he stays on top of it. With his optimism and strength the Wands figure beats down all problems. He does not try to compromise, accept difficulties, or even seek solutions. Instead he will keep on battling, for confrontation brings with it that rush of excitement. Among the things he beats down are his own doubts, suspicions, and uncertainties about himself and the future.

Reversed, the card shows that the problems mount. He can no longer keep them away by fighting off the opposition of others or conquering the difficulties in the situation and his own fears and contradictions. Perhaps he has begun to tire. The other cards may show him the way to free himself.

6: This card depicts heroic optimism. Facing some difficult situation, or seeking some important goal, the figure believes so strongly in his own success that he brings about his victory.

Already he wears a laurel wreath, while another hangs on his wand. A crowd of people walk alongside him. If 'nothing succeeds like success' then nothing inspires so much confidence as the person who believes that success is assured.

Reversed, the meaning turns upside down once again to denote pessimism, negativity, and a conviction of failure. This is not simply a mirror image. If success comes primarily from self-confidence (rather than say, hard work or careful planning) then once that confidence falters, it can easily slide into defeatism. Either right side up or reversed, the card implies a self-fulfilling prophecy. Believe in yourself and you will succeed. Doubt yourself and you will fail.

5: At first we see some boys fighting. When we look closer, we discover that no one is hurt and they are clearly enjoying themselves. The card signifies the love of competition and the joy of struggling to get ahead. It shows a great release of energy. Sometimes this comes after a long period of doubt or sadness when the person suddenly throws himself into life once more. Like some of the other Wands cards this love of conflict can become a trap. On the one hand the person may become a success and discover he misses the struggle. On the other, if he or she gets nowhere, enthusiasm can change to disillusionment.

Reversed, that sense of disillusionment is emphasized. The battle is no longer fun because the other people are not fighting 'fair'. The person may feel betrayed or cheated in some way. We sometimes see the 5 of Wands reversed in readings dealing with problems at work.

4: This card gives an image of joy and liberation. In its simplest form it shows a time in life when the sun shines and people celebrate their happiness. Since it depicts a couple rather than one person, it implies relationships, especially families. As in the 6, other people follow them. In that card, however, the crowd attached themselves to a charismatic leader. Here the people respond to a love of life.

If the card appears in a reading after a time of suffering it indicates the return of happiness. If it comes after arguments it shows people coming together again. Notice that the crowd is leaving a walled city which implies that people can leave their problems behind them. By an act of will, fuelled by the fire of optimism, they can discover freedom.

Reversed, the card remains positive but the situation loses some of that clarity. As with the Sun in the Major Arcana, the brightness becomes clouded over. It can become harder to dance away from the walled city.

3: We have seen that a number of Wands cards show youthful eagerness while others depict the burdens of success, as if the adult regrets having grown up. This card, however, shows someone who has established himself and who looks at the world – indeed at life – with satisfaction. Before him a group of boats sail out to sea. These symbolize new ideas. But he himself stays behind. He does not need to throw himself totally into new things or to give up his security for the sake of adventure.

We can also see the boats as *returning* rather than setting out. In this sense they symbolize memories. For a person struggling with the past the 3 of Wands implies the ability to look peacefully at memories and to allow the past to come home.

Reversed, the card indicates that the person no longer feels so sure of himself. He or she may lack the solid base to launch some new project. In terms of memory, the past is disturbing.

A simpler meaning is that since the card right side up shows someone alone, reversed it can indicate co-operation or help, especially in business.

2: Like the 3, this card symbolizes success. The figure stands on the wall of his castle and looks out at his land. He holds the world in his hand. But what a small world it is. The energy of Wands cannot feel comfortable with security. The figure appears bored, as if life has closed in around him. He yearns for the excitement of the 5, the adventure of the Knight. Compare him to the 4. There, the people are leaving the city in a group. Here, he stands alone behind the wall. This implies that success has cut him off from others. In fact, he cuts himself off because of his own belief and resentment over the fact that he has lost his freedom.

Reversed, the card shows that the person gives up security for the sake of adventure. Whatever is safe he leaves behind. Entering the unknown can bring great excitement and joy but also fear and trouble. Whether or not such a change is a good idea will depend on the other cards in the reading.

Ace: The Aces represent the pure energy of the suit and signify a time in someone's life when that energy dominates. The Ace of Wands, therefore, indicates a period of optimism, creative energy, sexual potency, and adventure. As with the 1, it signifies unity. In contrast to such cards as the 10, where the energy is directed to dealing with myriad concerns, the Ace shows the person focused on a single goal. All the Aces come to us as gifts from life. This is why the hand emerges from a cloud. It tells us that we cannot predict when the Ace of Wands will appear; we can only accept it when it does. The gift must be used wisely, particularly for starting projects or relationships, since the Fire energy will not last for ever.

Reversed, the card shows that the person finds it hard to hold on to the powerful Ace. Situations get out of control, the creative fire becomes less focused and breaks up in different directions. Sometimes the reversed Ace can suggest a misuse of the power the person has been given. He or she may try to dominate others, sometimes through sexual manipulation. More simply it says that the fire is burning out and the person should not depend on it.

CUPS

King: This card signifies someone creative and imaginative. Usually he has used his talents in some recognized profession. Like the other Kings he is successful and a respected member of the community. Like the King of Wands, however, this role may bother him. For just as the King of Wands had to restrict his love of adventure, so the King of Cups has narrowed his imagination to the professional or commercial context only. He is the successful lawyer who always wanted to be a poet. If the person concerned does work in the arts, then the King of Cups would indicate achievement and recognition. Emotionally he seems calm, even benevolent, but his outward appearance may conceal more complex emotions.

Reversed, the card indicates that he may use his creative talents to trick people or to get ahead without concern for principles. For an artist the reversed King means that his or her work has not matured. In emotional terms feelings of aggression have broken through the placid surface.

Queen: The Queen is one of the most powerful of the Minor Arcana cards. She is creative, with a strong will that enables her to develop her talents. She draws inspiration from her own life and from the world around her. More integrated into society than the King, she sits firmly on the land, a symbol of her connection with the 'real world' and other people. At the same time water flows into her dress, an image denoting that she does not suppress her emotions. Ultimately, her power and accomplishments are rooted in love.

Reversed, the card indicates that the creativity and willpower remain although the person can lose their connection with others. This can make him or her ambitious but dangerous. More simply, it can mean that the person has failed to reach the powerful level of the card right side up. The presence of the card at all in a reading though indicates that such a level is attainable.

Knight: This is the card of a dreamer, someone who moves slowly in the world, preferring to stay within himself, avoiding pressures at work or in relationships. And yet, he is still a knight, a figure of action, expected to take care of other people and to achieve things. People and responsibilities may call him from his dreams, as may sexual desire, since the Knight is a romantic figure in conflict with his own needs.

Reversed, the card indicates that this conflict becomes stronger. The Knight may rouse himself to action. Alternatively, others may push him to some sort of commitment, which he will then greatly resent. Pressed, he may turn sulky and manipulative.

Page: Unlike the Knight, the Page feels no pressure from outside but concerns himself only with his own thoughts and dreams. The card signifies the ability to step back and look at life. In a difficult situation it indicates a moment of calm. The Page examines the different sides of the problem without getting too upset by what he sees. Later, he will have to make decisions and choices.

This card can have a very specific meaning signifying psychic

KING of CUPS.
QUEEN of CUPS.
KNIGHT of CUPS.
PAGE of CUPS.
X
IX
VIII
VII
VI
V
IV
III
II
ACE of CUPS.

ability. As a Page the person has not developed this talent. It has just begun to emerge. (The High Priestess would indicate a powerful potential. The Queen of Cups would show greater development.)

Reversed, the card can signify, on the one hand, impulsive action, doing something you really want to without giving any thought to the consequences. On the other hand, it may indicate that the Page's sense of calm has been lost. The things in his cup – relationships, questions about the future, and so on – disturb him. He believes he should do something but does not know quite what.

10: This card denotes a happy family and a home filled with love, trust, and celebration. It does not mean that there will be no problems. The people may suffer but they recognize that life remains wonderful. They have each other and this enables them to see the rainbow that comes after the storm. The two adults look up at the rainbow but the children dance without noticing it. The card may symbolize a secure childhood.

Reversed, the card indicates that the domestic environment has gone through an upset of some kind. The people quarrel and no longer trust each other. It may also mean that the person lacked security as a child.

9: This is a card of good times, of parties, excellent food and drink, entertainment, and romantic adventures without commitment. The value of this may depend on the other cards in the reading. If nothing demands serious attention, the 9 signifies pleasure. If the person is neglecting something, however, the 9 becomes an indication of escapism.

Reversed, this card is, unusually, more powerful. Waite, the deck's designer, says that it signifies 'truth, loyalty, and liberty'. The person turns away from superficial fun in order to find some deeper meaning to life.

8: This card shows a man walking up a hill under a full moon. At the bottom stand eight cups. The scene represents the ability to leave something behind in order to go on to new concerns. The cups have not fallen (as in the 5). There has been no disaster. The person has simply recognized that the time has come to move

Facing page: The suit of Cups

on. The picture appears to show an eclipse with the moon moving across the sun. Since the Sun card symbolizes action and the Moon withdrawal, it denotes a shift in someone's life. From being very involved with doing things and with others, the person now needs quiet and a chance to be alone. This becomes stronger if the card appears in a reading with the Hermit.

Reversed, the card indicates two possibilities. Most often it tells the person to bear with the situation. This is not the time to leave or to try something new. Alternatively, it can mean the inability to leave. In many situations – a relationship that has gone wrong or a job without a future – he or she may want to leave but lack the courage. To choose between these two meanings, compare them with the other cards.

7: Cups' energy contains imagination but finds it difficult to take action. In this card we see the daydreamer, his mind filled with visions. Some of these are things he desires: fame, wealth, and love. Others, such as the mysterious hooded figure, are simply fantasies which make life exciting. Other daydreams may frighten, such as the dragon or the snake. What unites them all is their lack of connection to the person's life.

Reversed, the card shows that action replaces vague daydreaming. The reversed 7 does not mean that the person must give up his or her fantasies. Instead it tells him or her to decide which fantasies matter and to take practical steps to make them come alive.

6: This card shows an older child giving a present to a younger one. This represents a protected and secure relationship. No decisions have to be made and the subject has nothing to worry about, for the other person will take care of everything. The card may refer to actual childhood, though it more often denotes a nostalgic memory of childhood as a time free of problems. Such fantasies may make it difficult for a person to do something new or to form an adult relationship.

As a picture of a current relationship the 6 of Cups can indicate that one person acts the role of 'big brother' or 'big sister', allowing the other to be dependent.

Reversed, the card no longer denotes nostalgia but instead a looking to the future (or the present) rather than the past. This can mean accepting responsibility instead of longing for someone else to solve all the problems.

5: This card deals with the problem of loss. The person looks sadly at the three spilled cups. Something that once existed is no longer, or something long hoped for has failed to materialize and the person must now confront his or her reactions to this failure. How did the cups get spilled? Were they knocked over through carelessness?

The person's attention focuses on the loss. Two cups, however, still stand. These symbolize what remains of the situation. They may also represent what is really important in the person's life, in other words, what cannot be knocked over.

Reversed, the card denotes a shifting of attention to the two cups still standing. The person begins to get over the loss and to take steps to carry on with what really matters. In terms of the symbolism, he or she turns away from the spilled cups, picks up the two that are still standing and carries them over the bridge back to the house.

4: The 4 shows an image of apathy. Three cups stand before the person, indicating what life has already given him. Instead of appreciating these gifts, however, he sits under his tree, bored. Now a hand comes from a cloud to offer him a new cup, symbol of new experience and new possibilities. It resembles the Ace of Cups, which implies that the fourth cup will bring him happiness if he can only stir himself to accept it. This means getting up and doing something. The person can take hold of the cup by taking action. In a reading this card tells him or her to look around. Some opportunity hangs in the air, waiting. It may mean work, a relationship, or an adventure but the person's apathy keeps him or her from seeing it.

Reversed, the card has a very direct meaning. The person shakes off his apathy, gets up from his tree and takes hold of the opportunity.

3: This lovely card symbolizes harmony and friendship. The women dance together, raising their cups in a toast to life. In a reading the card indicates support from friends, people who share both life's burdens and its happinesses. The women's bodies entwine as a symbol of co-operation and shared experience. This card sometimes appears in a position signifying someone's hopes. In complex relationships between several people, the card can represent the ideal image which the person would like to see in reality.

Reversed, the card indicates that this ideal is threatened or has been lost. People find it hard to work together or to trust one another. Resentment may take the place of co-operation or the person may feel a lack of support from friends.

A lighter meaning for the reversed 3 is that of physical pleasures but without the deeper emotional commitment that is shown in the card right side up.

2: This card indicates a strong relationship, especially the beginning of one. Two young people pledge themselves to each other. The card symbolizes not only commitment but also the romance and excitement of 'young love' (which may come to people at any age). In the Lovers the angel appears over the people's heads. Here a winged lion rises above a caduceus (a staff entwined by two serpents bearing a pair of wings at the top and carried by Hermes), a symbol of healing which is used by the medical profession. Both cards indicate that two people can create a life together that is more fulfilled than their lives alone. The lion symbolizes sex; the wings, spirit. Love and commitment transform the sex drive. In a reading about a break-up the 2 of Cups can show the possibility of a new relationship.

Reversed, the 2 of Cups indicates problems in a relationship as do the reversed Lovers. It can mean a lack of trust or commitment. Another meaning is infatuation.

Ace: This card shows us the gift of Cups: joy, love, and the healing power of the imagination. The picture, with the dove and the Christian wafer, is that of the holy grail, the magical cup of the King Arthur legend. In the story the grail cup came to a wasteland of sickness where nothing would grow and the king lay in a coma. Just as the grail restored the king and the land, so the Ace of Cups, the gift of joy, brings wholeness and new happiness to a person's life.

Reversed, the card indicates that overflowing happiness changing to bitterness. People quarrel and no longer trust one another. Sometimes the reversed Ace means that the happiness exists but that it has not been recognized or accepted.

SWORDS

King: Perhaps the strongest of the Kings, the King of Swords is someone with a truly dominating personality. Intelligent and forceful, he approaches situations and people with an air of authority. He can be judgmental, even dogmatic, though at his best he remains fair and principled. He knows too that he must act on his decisions. Along with his authority, he assumes a high degree of responsibility. And yet, just as the King of Wands can become intolerant of those less sure of themselves, so the King of Swords can look down on people less intelligent.

Reversed, the card shows that intolerance increased. The person becomes dogmatic and dismissive of those who cannot compete intellectually. The reversed King may show someone eager for power and not too worried about how he gets it.

Queen: Sadder, but in a sense purer than the King, the Queen holds her sword straight up as a symbol of truth and wisdom (compare the sword of Justice). In contrast, the King's sword tilts because of his tendency to use his intellect to dominate others. In many cases the Queen's wisdom has come from suffering. The card may even symbolize a widow. Her powerful mind and will, however, have allowed her to face those troubles with honesty and to learn from them. She teaches us to accept life as it is.

Reversed, the card indicates that she loses that strength of character and may give herself over to self-pity. Alternatively, the reversed Queen can denote a nasty or prejudiced attitude about someone or something.

Knight: The emphasis shifts here from Swords as intellect to Swords as conflict. The Knight is brave, aggressive, and sometimes reckless. When faced with trouble he wants to ride directly into the storm, ignoring subtleties or careful planning. He may tend to ride roughshod over other people but he is always honest and at least as hard on himself as on anyone else. His eagerness can create problems, for he sometimes jumps into situations where a second look might have held him back.

Reversed, the card can have several meanings. On one level it indicates wildness, the reckless side of the Knight carried to an extreme. He may become more aggressive, tending to attack people, perhaps as a way of not facing up to his own doubts. Another possibility is that he has charged at someone or something too powerful and has been knocked off his horse.

Page: A much lighter and gentler figure than the Knight, the Page does not charge at problems or at other people. Instead he prefers to remove himself. We see him on a hilltop, detached from whatever is going on below. He is also, however, looking over his shoulder, holding his sword at the ready. He hasn't really escaped trouble, only managed to distance himself from it, and he waits nervously to see if it will come after him.

With his detached attitude the Page will sometimes look at other people's lives and troubles (perhaps even his own life) as something curious and interesting but not real or to be taken seriously.

Reversed, the card shows that the Page tries so hard to keep himself away from trouble that he may become suspicious of everyone around him. The reversed Page indicates nervousness and anxiety.

10: At first glance this card depicts total disaster, even violent death. The very extremity of the picture, however, gives a hint of its true meaning. One sword is enough to kill a person. Here ten stick in his back, even one in his ear. The picture, then, symbolizes hysteria, an over-exaggerated response to real problems. Notice also the clear skies and calm waters underneath the clouds. Things are not so disastrous as they seem.

Reversed, the card shows that matters improve but not permanently. Just as the mind can dramatize troubles, so a person can wrongly assume that a temporary respite means that all their problems have disappeared. In a reading the 10 of Swords says that things will become easier but that the person must use this opportunity to make real changes. Otherwise, the same difficulties will return.

Facing page: The suit of Swords

9: The 9 is one of the most difficult, yet often one of the most important cards that can appear in a reading. It shows us a

KING of SWORDS.
QUEEN of SWORDS.
KNIGHT of SWORDS.
PAGE of SWORDS.
X
IX
VIII
VII
VI
V
IV
III
II
ACE of SWORDS.

picture of true sorrow, as if the woman's pain has woken her in the middle of the night. The roses on her blanket denote passionate emotion but also love, for the card sometimes refers to feeling pain for someone else.

Pay special attention to this card in any position where it refers to the past. The 9 of Swords sometimes exposes hidden or repressed sorrow. For instance, if the person's parents divorced when he or she was a child, when representing the past the card can mean that the person is still affected by the trauma.

Reversed, the meaning shifts more to repression than sorrow. The person feels a sense of confusion and imprisonment. These things all come from not confronting some hidden fear.

8: Like the Devil reversed, the 8 shows us a picture of someone trapped. The ropes hold her, the swords (a symbol of danger) surround her. Behind her rises a castle (an image of other people's power over her) and she stands in the mud, denoting shame. But look carefully. The ropes do not bind her legs, there are no swords in front of her and there is no one from the castle to guard her. Just as in the Devil card, she can walk away, if only she realized. What stops her is the blindfold which signifies confusion. Thus, the card describes a feeling of helplessness although the way out is revealed if she can only think things through and see the real possibilities.

Reversed, the person takes the first steps to freedom. She or he understands the situation and does something about it.

7: Here someone in a difficult situation tries to accomplish something. He is very pleased with what he has done. We see the figure grinning as he makes off with five of the seven swords. In fact he has not really changed anything. The card, therefore, indicates action without planning, a bold move that doesn't produce solid results. The 7 of Swords often acts as a warning. It may appear as a counter to the Fool, saying that the Fool's impulsiveness is not what the person needs. First he or she must work out a plan.

The card also represents doing things alone and refusing help from others. A further meaning is that of craftiness, a tendency to conceal one's plans and emotions, sometimes even when this is unnecessary.

Reversed, the card indicates that the person seeks the advice and help of others. The value of this advice will depend on the other cards. If he or she cannot do things alone, then the 7 reversed is a positive step. Sometimes, however, he or she *must* cope alone and in these circumstances all that advice will just confuse them. The 7 of Swords reversed may also signify gossip rather than advice.

6: The traditional meanings of this card include 'journey by water, route, way'. Although these remain valid, Pamela Smith's picture implies much more. No one talks to each other; the woman sits shrouded with the cargo of swords in front of her. The card indicates the carrying of emotional burdens, in other words, depression, where the person accepts a sort of half-alive state rather than disturbing the boat by trying to remove the swords (that is, bring the problems to the surface). The silence represents a relationship or a situation in which people have stopped talking to each other. It may indicate some very specific issue that no one is prepared to discuss openly.

Reversed, the card can have several meanings. If it refers to a journey, then reversed it indicates delays, storms, or other difficulties. As an emotional image it says that the person is doing their best to shake off the depression. Another reading is that of communication, where some delicate matter that everyone has tried to ignore is brought out into the open.

5: Another of the most difficult cards, the 5 of Swords symbolizes defeat, weakness, and humiliation. The figure holding the swords represents an enemy, either an actual person or maybe a situation that overpowers the subject of the reading. The other two people have not only lost a battle, they have lost their self-respect and, maybe, their hopes. The reader needs to balance this card against others in order to show the person a way out of such pessimism.

Sometimes this card acts as a warning, telling the subject to avoid a battle that cannot be won.

Reversed, the card indicates that the defeat remains, although it is also possible to say that it shows the person attempting to recover from the setback. Whatever battles the person has lost, new opportunities will come.

4: This card denotes a tendency to retreat in times of trouble. We see a knight lying asleep in a church. Many people, especially those who regard themselves as powerful, optimistic, or domineering, cannot accept weakness or doubt in themselves. If life becomes difficult, they prefer to isolate themselves rather than appear helpless. Sometimes the card indicates a period of rest and implies that after it the person will return to the outside world. At other times the isolation can take over. In this state of mind the person pushes away anyone who tries to help.

Reversed, the card shows that the person returns from isolation. This may come from their own efforts or, like the prince kissing Sleeping Beauty, because someone has got past the barriers erected and insisted on helping.

3: Like the 9, the 3 is a card of sorrow. We see literally a heart in pain, pierced by swords. The specific cause of the pain may show up in the other cards. The Lovers reversed, for instance, would refer to the break-up of a relationship. (You might want to discuss possible causes with the subject.) Either way, the 3 of Swords (like the 9) does not show the event so much as the emotions produced by it.

The card carries a certain calm as well. By accepting the sorrow into our hearts we can overcome it, perhaps even transform it through the power of love (the appearance of the 3 of Cups in the reading would emphasize this possibility). If the 3 of Swords appears, look at the other cards. Do they show a way in which the person can overcome the pain?

Reversed, the person tries to push the pain away and not to think about it. Often this prolongs the problems, for healing must begin with acceptance.

2: The 2 of Swords shows another blindfolded figure. Here, the symbol indicates keeping people at a distance. With her swords (her emotional armour) the woman creates a fence around herself. The blindfold means that she makes no distinction between friend and enemy but simply keeps everyone away. By behaving in this way she maintains her emotional balance at a difficult time in her life. But that balance is very precarious. Sitting rigidly, with the swords on her shoulders, she can easily tip backwards into the emotional waters.

Reversed, the fence comes down. The person has taken the blindfold off and dropped the swords, thus allowing others to approach. Or, the problems may become too much for her.

Ace: With the Ace we return to Swords as denoting intellect. The upright sword symbolizes truth. It pierces through the centre of a crown. This means that the mind allows us to see beyond the immediate situation and attain a higher awareness. In a reading the Ace denotes powerful emotion but also rational analysis, understanding, and mental dominance. The hand grasps the sword very tightly. Like the others, this Ace is a gift, in some ways the most powerful. But that mental power is hard to control.

Reversed, the hand slips and the emotions run away with the person. Love, hate, and anger all take over as the rational mind loses its ability to see the truth and keep things in perspective. Like some other cards, the reversed Ace acts as a warning. The person needs to keep a grip on things.

PENTACLES

King: Pentacles are the most stable of the four suits, showing the 'real world': nature, money, and work. Successful, comfortable and proud of his achievements, the King does not feel confined like the King of Wands, nor creatively repressed like the King of Cups. Nor does he seek to dominate or direct like the King of Swords. He simply enjoys his physical comforts, his status in the community, his pride in his achievements – in short, his life.

Reversed, the card indicates a lack of achievement. The person may feel dissatisfied with life or disappointed in him or herself. Right side up or reversed, the King of Pentacles needs success.

Queen: The Queen shows an appreciation of the inner quality of the suit, especially of nature. Less concerned with pride, achievement, or social position than the King, she enjoys life and herself. She has found her rhythm with the world and does not worry too much about success or status. She believes in herself and the magic of her life.

The rabbit in the picture stands for fertility. The Queen of Pentacles is often a mother. Like the Queen of Wands she

KING of PENTACLES
QUEEN of PENTACLES
KNIGHT of PENTACLES
PAGE of PENTACLES
X
IX
VIII
VII
VI
IV
III
II
ACE of PENTACLES

enjoys sex, though she is less forceful sexually than her Wands sister.

Reversed, the Queen of Pentacles represents a loss of harmony. Something is not going right and the person finds it difficult to appreciate the simple things in life. More specifically it indicates a lack of confidence in a particular situation. The person needs to restore their self-trust.

Knight: The Knight of Pentacles is practical, hardworking, and absorbed in his job. He is a perfectionist, paying great attention to detail in his work and to doing things correctly. Unlike the Knight of Wands, he does not seek adventure. He does not charge at problems as does the Knight of Swords, nor does he follow his own dreams like the Knight of Cups. Instead, he does his job. Unfortunately, he can become dull, stuck in a rut and afraid, or simply unable to see opportunities or take chances. He may need other influences to shake him loose from his dedication to detail.

Reversed, the card goes in two directions. It can refer to the person becoming irresponsible or reckless. More often, however, it denotes someone cut off from the work which gives his or her life meaning. Examples of this would be a mother whose children have grown up, or an employee who gives his life to the company and does not know what to do with his retirement.

Page: The Page of Pentacles symbolizes the student. Absorbed and fascinated by his studies, he looks at nothing but his pentacle, giving little thought to practical questions outside his work. He is not a dreamer though. He puts great effort into his own concerns. He simply. does not worry very much about anything else.

Obviously, in readings the card will not always refer to an actual student. Symbolically, the Page of Pentacles represents someone approaching any activity with fascination, total absorption, and a lack of interest in financial rewards or public approval. We may see him as an idealist but in fact he simply does not care about anything other than his 'studies'.

Reversed, the fascination remains but it loses the grounding in hard work. Instead, the Page of Pentacles follows whims and idle distractions and goes wherever his interest takes him.

Facing page: The suit of Pentacles

10: Like the 10 of Cups reversed, the 10 of Pentacles represents home and family. Whereas the Cups card celebrated love, the Pentacles card denotes security and material comfort. The people are well-dressed and live in a substantial house. But the 10 also hints that they find this security boring. Magic symbols fill the card. The ten pentacles are arranged in the mystical Tree of Life pattern. A mysterious visitor sits outside the gate and a magic wand (the only one in the Minor Arcana) rests against the wall. The people do not see these things, however. Nor do they talk to one another. Their lives are magical but they think of them as dull and ordinary.

Reversed, the card indicates that the person rebels against security and takes risks. He or she gambles or acts recklessly for the sake of adventure.

9: This card symbolizes discipline. The woman stands in her own garden. She is successful, as the pentacles growing on the bushes show. She stands alone because she has done it by herself. In a reading the card tells the person to rely on her or himself rather than on outside help.

The falcon on her wrist denotes desire, imagination, the mind, talent, and so on. The hood stands for training rather than repression. By disciplining herself and developing her abilities she has made something valuable of her life.

Reversed, the card indicates that lack of discipline brings failure. The person abandons projects rather than overcoming obstacles. The card can mean laziness or indicate someone who cannot decide what really matters.

8: Pentacles insist on the value of work. In contrast to the excitement of Wands or the romance of Cups, they show us people finding satisfaction in their work. This card shows an apprentice, someone learning a skill. He makes pentacle after pentacle, unconcerned with financial reward or fame. In a reading, especially one concerning career or ambition, this card tells someone to concentrate on basic techniques and skills. It also tells the person to feel joy in what he or she is doing.

Reversed, the card denotes that the person becomes impatient and cannot concentrate. It may also indicate an envy of other people's success.

7: Like the 9, this card represents satisfaction. The person has worked hard (applying both the discipline of the 9 and the concentration of the 8) and can now step back and look at what he or she has accomplished, whether this is in terms of their career, a particular project, or their life as a whole. The card also implies that the person has started something (such as a business) and can now step back and let it continue on its own without fear of it collapsing.

Reversed, the card indicates dissatisfaction because work (or life in general, a love affair, or any other enterprise) is not leading anywhere or developing.

6: A complex card, the 6 of Pentacles refers in the first instance to gifts. If the *beggars* symbolize the subject, then he or she can expect a gift or help of some kind from someone in an established position. The gift will not be large – we see the merchant carefully measuring out the coins. However, if the *merchant* symbolizes the subject, then he or she will be in a position to help someone else.

The card can also describe a particular kind of relationship where the partners have got into a rigid pattern or where one person dominates the other. Sometimes the beggars represent both people in the relationship and the merchant (like the Devil, though not as extreme) symbolizes the situation itself, which is unfulfilling for both of them.

Reversed, in terms of giving, the card can denote selfishness. It can also mean that pride prevents the person from asking for help. In terms of relationships the rigid situation described above becomes disrupted and the people have the opportunity to stop playing the roles of merchant and beggar and to become more equal.

5: As the picture indicates, this card first of all shows problems such as ill health and money troubles. It also represents a strong bond, for the two people struggle together, sharing their hardships. They are surviving, even if they are not comfortable. Sometimes they can become dependent on trouble, afraid that success or relief will break up their relationship. In a reading, this card can help the person recognize such fears.

Reversed, the card may mean healing or relief from troubles.

However, it sometimes goes in the opposite direction and survival becomes more difficult. This may not be so bad. Like someone losing a low-paying job, it may give the person the incentive to make something better of his or her life.

4: This card shows a miser. He holds on tightly to what he's got, deriving security and satisfaction from his possessions. Emotionally it can refer to a person concerned primarily with himself.

In a difficult situation the card can indicate someone holding himself together. If everything around him becomes chaotic, he needs to create a structure in his life and immediate surroundings. The card can, therefore, symbolize routine, fixed patterns, rules, and anything that brings order.

Reversed, the card shows that the miser becomes generous. Emotionally, the person gives more of himself to others. In terms of structure, he or she becomes less rigid.

3: Just as the 8 showed an apprentice, the 3 of Pentacles gives us a picture of a master, someone skilled and successful. He is a creator, carving statues in the church. A monk and an architect help him. They symbolize spiritual values and training, two qualities necessary for important work. In readings, this card will often indicate that the person has reached a high level of ability and accomplishment in work or career. Or, as a card of the future, it says that the person can attain that level. This card can justify a person's ambition.

Reversed, the card indicates mediocrity, primarily in a work context but sometimes in life in general. The presence of the 3 of Pentacles at all, however, suggests that hard work (as well as training and spiritual values) can overcome that mediocrity.

2: This card symbolizes a playful approach to life. Many things are happening but the person manages to juggle them all, keeping them in the air, while he dances to his own music. Like the 9 of Cups, it signifies a good time. People sometimes consider this card very valuable in a reading.

Reversed, the gaiety becomes forced. The person pretends to take everything lightly but underneath the problems are mounting. It can denote social pressure not to make a fuss.

Ace: The Ace is the gift of Pentacles denoting comfort, security, wealth, satisfying work, and opportunities for advancement, the joy of nature, and a pleasant life. Like the other Aces, this gift is never permanent but we can certainly enjoy it when it comes. A path leads out of the garden to the mountains and the unknown. Security here does not confine the person as in the 2 of Wands but gives them the opportunity to develop in a safe situation and then to go further.

Reversed, the Ace signifies material comforts and the problems arising from them: greed, selfishness, mistrust, and an over-dependence on security and wealth.

The reversed Ace can also mean leaving the garden – giving up a safe situation in order to look for something greater in life. As usual, the specific interpretation will depend on the other cards in the reading.

READINGS

The Tarot (and many other forms of divination) often give several possible meanings for a particular card. Many people starting out find this confusing. Do not let it worry you overmuch, for as you become more practised, you will find it much easier to choose the most appropriate interpretation. When you begin you will probably want to consult the book meanings for each card. Do so by all means but make sure to leave room for your own impressions, especially your reactions to the pictures. Explore also the possibility that *several* meanings might apply, even some that may appear contradictory. Human beings are highly complex and can often go (or try to go) in several directions at once. This holds particularly true for cards depicting a person's attitude to a situation.

While each card has its own meanings, the real truth of the reading lies in the combinations formed by the cards as the meanings of each card will affect all the others. Such combinations will be obvious. For instance, if the card of the present situation is the Devil (people trapped in an unpleasant situation) and the outcome is the 4 of Wands (people joyously moving into the open), then the reading tells you that the people concerned will find a way to break free of their problems. Or suppose someone recently divorced asks for a reading. The first card is the 5 of Cups. This shows their sadness at the end of the marriage. The last card, however, is the 2 of Cups indicating that he or she will begin a new relationship.

In considering combinations pay attention to the pictures. In the example just given, notice in the 5 of Cups that two cups stand behind the sorrowful figure. This relates to the 2 of Cups at the end of the reading and tells the person that the new relationship is likely to be with someone he or she already knows. The new possibility is there but the person cannot see it as long as he or she remains focused on the loss – the three spilled cups. As you become more experienced, you will notice such things naturally.

Like many Tarot commentaries this book gives reversed (upside down) meanings for each card. Some people find reversed cards hard to interpret. Try to think of them as a block or interference with the natural working out of the card. Use the interpretations given here as guidelines to discover how the reversed meanings derive from those of the cards right side up.

People often ask what period of time a Tarot reading describes. There is no fixed rule. Firstly, it depends on the complexity of the question. If the person asks, 'Will I get the job?', then the reading will cover a short time. If the question is, 'Should I go back to school to learn a profession?', the reading will describe a longer timespan. In general, the deeper a reading penetrates into the person's life, the longer it applies. Use your common sense and your own intuition about the situation and what the cards are saying about it.

When you begin your work with the cards, get yourself two notebooks. In the first record each of the readings you do, along with the date and a few words about the subject, the situation, and the interpretation. If you stay in touch with the person, you can then compare subsequent events with what you saw in the cards. Also, if the same person comes back to you, you can check back in your notebook on previous readings. If someone comes back several times, one or two cards will, occasionally, gain special significance. One woman came to me a number of times for advice concerning her relationship with her boyfriend. The 10 of Wands appeared in almost every reading. It signified her willingness to take all the burdens of the relationship on herself. In another case the King of Swords appeared in a woman's reading as the 'near future'. The next time the card showed up in the position of 'self'. In her following reading it appeared as 'recent past'. The problem symbolized by the card had approached, occupied her attention and then moved away into the past. The three readings took place over several weeks.

In the second notebook record your own observations about the cards. Set several pages aside for each one. Write down your ideas and your impressions of the pictures. As you discover new things about the cards, add them to your commentary. In a separate section write down any special thoughts you have on the cards in general, or on readings, together with any stories or fantasies told with the cards, drawings inspired by them and so on. In time you will have created your own Tarot.

READINGS: BASIC TECHNIQUES

To begin the readings you need to choose the person's 'significator' which will represent him or her. The reader removes it from the deck before the person shuffles the cards and will usually not interpret this card. Many methods exist for choosing the significator. Here is a simple one:

The significator will frequently come from one of the court cards. Pages symbolize a child of either sex, Knights a young adult of either sex who has not chosen a definite direction in life. Queens represent a mature woman, Kings a mature man. Choose the category that fits the person and then remove those four cards from the deck. For instance, for a married woman with children you would probably take out the four Queens. Then ask her to choose one of the four to represent herself. Do not explain the symbolism of each of the cards but tell her to make a choice based on her feelings about the picture. When she has chosen the significator, replace the other three cards in the deck. If you do a series of readings for someone, you will probably want to use the same significator each time.

When you have laid the significator on the table, give the cards to the person to shuffle. Make sure that he or she shuffles them thoroughly, face down, and that some of the cards get turned round. This can be done by spreading the cards all over the table and then bringing them back together.

If the person wishes to ask a specific question, he or she should keep it in mind while shuffling. If the subject simply wants to see what the Tarot will say, he or she should try to clear their mind of extraneous thoughts and focus on the act of shuffling the cards.

Ask the person to tell you the question they have in mind. This serves two purposes. First, it helps the subject of the reading to clarify the question in his or her own mind. Second, it tells you where to focus your concentration. Some people are reluctant to voice their question. They consider this 'cheating' because they expect the diviner to see everything in the cards. You *can*, of course, discover the question from the cards. For instance, the Lovers would signify romantic issues, a number of Pentacles cards would suggest a question concerning work. But a Tarot reading is not a game or a stunt. The person should come not to test the psychic powers of the reader but to seek advice. A reader who knows the question in advance can give much better advice than one who has to guess at it.

After the deck has been shuffled, ask the person to place it face down on the table. Using the left hand the subject should cut the deck to the left, then, from the left-hand pile, cut the deck again to give three piles. With your own left hand place the pile on the right (the bottom pile) on top of the middle pile and then the two together on top of the remaining pile. With your right hand turn the cards face up, from the top, in the various positions of the spread (described below). Turn the cards over like the pages of a book and make sure you do not flip them, reversing the top and bottom. This way, right-side-up cards will remain so and reversed cards will stay reversed. You can now begin your interpretation.

SPREADS

Some Tarot readers, especially those who use the pictures to stimulate psychic awareness, prefer to turn over cards in no particular pattern. Most people, however, like to place the cards in a definite form, called a 'spread' or a 'layout'. There are a great many spreads but most work in much the same way. Each position carries its own meaning. Some examples are 'recent past', 'obstacles', 'other people', and so on. Very often the last card will bear the title 'outcome' and will show the likely result of all the other influences. The meaning of a specific card depends on the card itself and on its position.

Three-Card Spreads: We will begin our look at layouts with two simple ones, both of which use only three cards. This will help you get used to interpreting the cards. For both, lay the three cards in a row underneath the significator (see Figure 25).

In the first method, card 2, the centre card, represents the current situation, the problems and opportunities facing the person. Card 1, on the left, indicates past experience, something that has led up to the current situation. Card 3, on the right, shows the future. This does not mean that it gives a fixed prediction but that it is simply an indication of the way things are heading. The person can change the development by his or her actions.

We will look briefly at an example (see Figure 25, example 1). A young woman has found herself in conflict with her parents. She wishes to understand the situation better and so asks the cards, choosing for her significator the Knight of Cups.

The 6 of Cups tells the woman something about her past. Her parents have sheltered her and treated her as a little girl. She has allowed this, accepting their protection and control. The 5 of Wands, denoting the present situation, shows the current conflict. It also describes that situation as healthy and a necessary release from a confining relationship. As the projected future, the 3 of Cups shows a renewed closeness with her parents but this time as equals. Therefore, the reading tells the woman that she is doing the right thing, for the present conflict will lead to a better relationship in the future.

The other three-card method involves choices. Again the card in the middle depicts the current situation. This time, however, the cards on either side of it show two of the choices available to the person. We will look at another example (see Figure 25, example 2). A man has worked a number of years at a job. Recently, he has found himself bored, despite advancement. He is considering looking for something else, possibly a whole new line of work. He chooses the King of Wands for his significator and, when he has mixed the cards, the reader turns up the line shown in the bottom diagram on page 118.

The centre card shows both his success and his dissatisfaction. It describes his feeling that life has closed in around him. The Knight of Wands on the left shows one choice. He can break loose and leave his job. The card tells him that this will bring

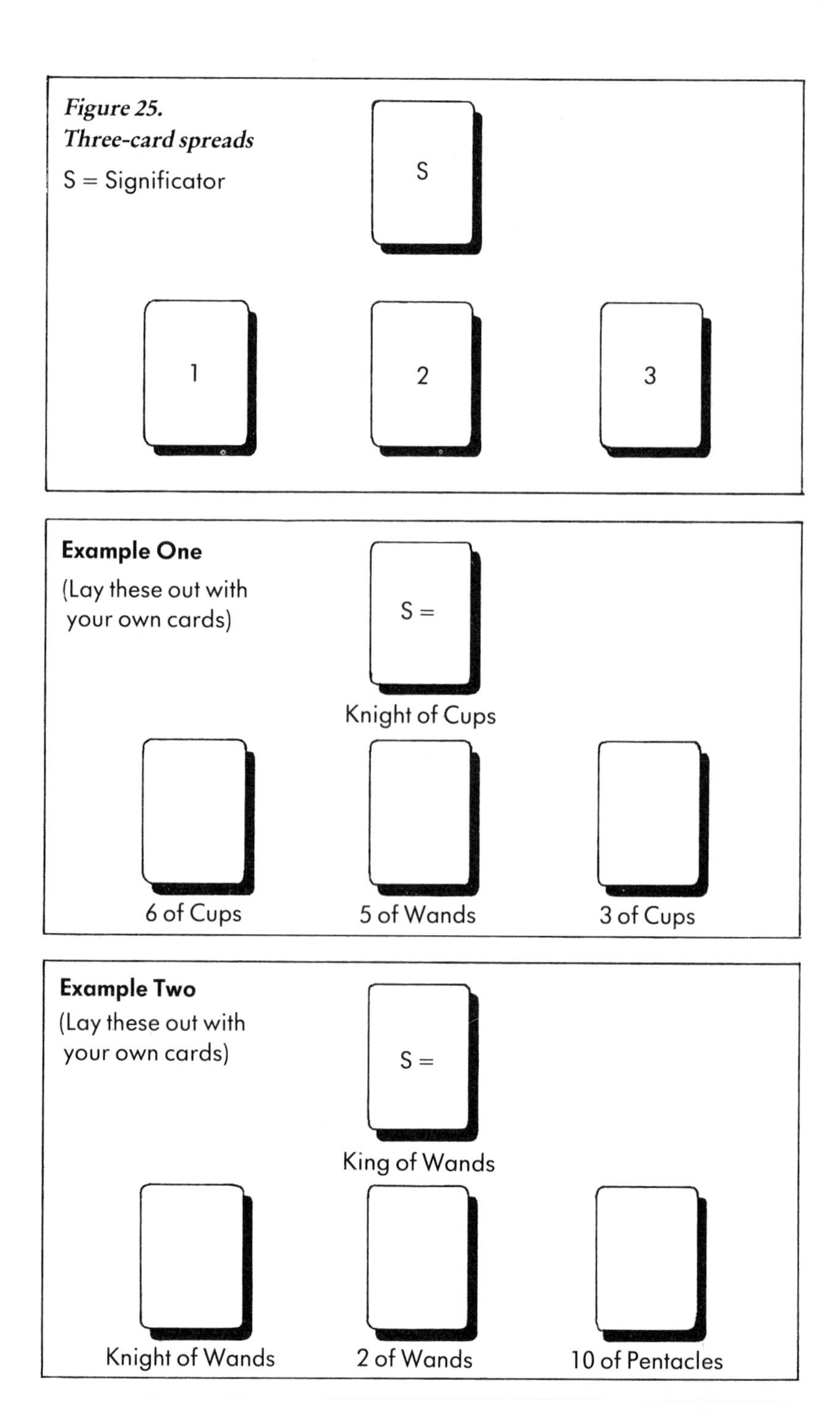
Figure 25.
Three-card spreads
S = Significator
S
1
2
3
Example One
(Lay these out with your own cards)
S =
Knight of Cups
6 of Cups
5 of Wands
3 of Cups
Example Two
(Lay these out with your own cards)
S =
King of Wands
Knight of Wands
2 of Wands
10 of Pentacles

excitement in his life. But it also will mean an unknown future and possibly that he will neglect his responsibility to his family. The 10 of Pentacles, on the other side, emphasizes security, success, and a good life in terms of material comforts. It also, however, shows the possibility of continued boredom. The 10 of Pentacles contains its own magic but the man will have to work harder to find it – and it is not the magic of adventure.

The reading states the problem strongly, showing him that there is no easy choice. Still, he may wish for more information about the consequences of the two sides. For this, he will need to do a longer reading that shows more detail. He might use this to ask a question derived from the three-card reading. For instance, he might do a Celtic Cross (see below) on the question, 'How will my life develop if I choose the Knight of Wands?'

The layouts just described are only two of the many using three cards. A look at other Tarot books will give you more ideas. If, like many people, you wish to make up your own spreads, you can begin with three cards. Experiment with different meanings for the positions. Another example is self (card 1), situation (card 2), and other people (card 3). When you have tried out some three-card layouts you can go on to more complex patterns.

Celtic Cross: Probably the most popular Tarot spread, the Celtic Cross, appears in many books, usually with slight variations. The version given here is one I have used for many years (see Figure 26). After a person has mixed and cut the cards, turn over the first card and lay it on top of the significator. Lay the second card horizontally across the first. Turn over cards 3–10 in the pattern around the first two.

Cards 1 and 2 form the 'small cross' or 'centre' cards. Cards 3–6 are the 'cross', while cards 7–10 form the 'staff'. The meanings of the positions are as follows:

1. The cover card – this shows the basic situation, the central issue.

2. The crossing card – this card joins with the first to state the concerns of the reading. Sometimes it acts as an opposition to

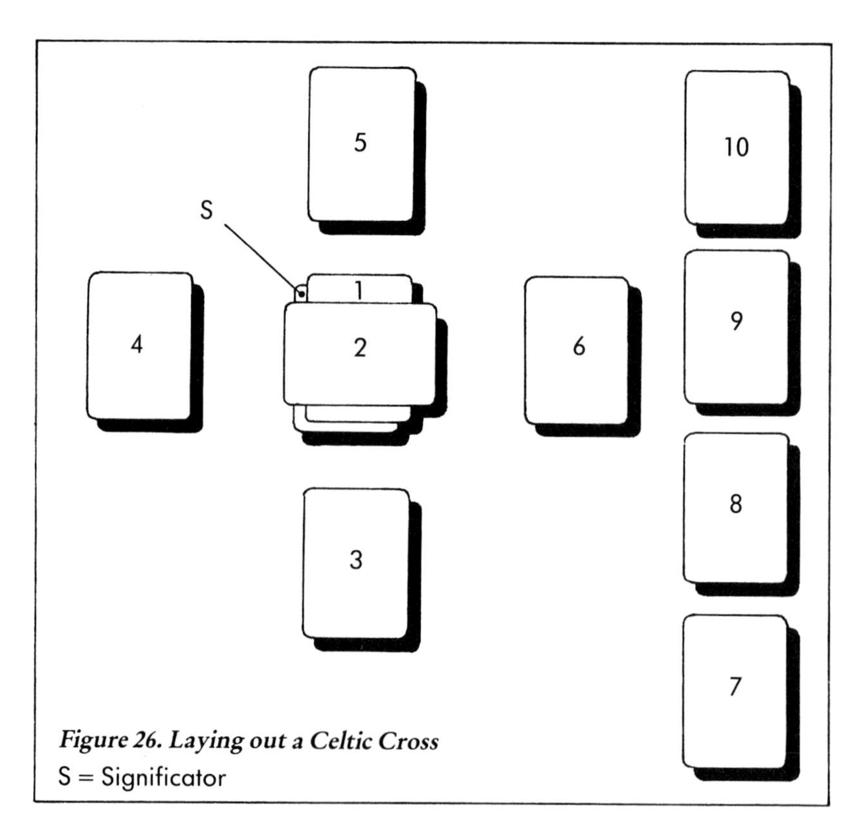

Figure 26. Laying out a Celtic Cross
S = Significator

the first card but it may also show some result that has developed from the first card.

An example of opposition: the question concerns work and the 8 of Pentacles appears as the cover card. This indicates the need to develop skills and work hard. The crossing card is the 7 of Cups. This shows that a tendency to daydream and fantasize distracts the person from the steadiness of the 8 of Pentacles.

An example of development: The Lovers reversed as the centre card shows problems in a relationship. Crossing this, the 9 of Swords indicates the sadness the person feels at this.

3. Basis – this card depicts some experience, usually in the past, that acts as the root or cause of the current situation. It may indicate a specific event or a more general condition that has led to the developments shown in the two centre cards. Sometimes this card will reach deeply into the person's life. Once, in a reading about a woman's sexual problems, the Emperor in the basis brought up a stifling relationship with her father.

4. Recent past – this card does not reach as far back as the basis. It indicates what has been happening recently in terms of the person's question. It may show something that has finished but still affects him or her. Or, it may show a continuing situation; in this case, the influence will probably come to an end soon.

5. Possible outcome – this card shows the general way things are heading. In contrast to the last card, the outcome, it is less specific and less definite. For instance, an outcome of the Page of Wands might indicate a decision taken about something, while Strength as the possible outcome shows the person generally feeling strong within himself or herself.

6. Near future – this card indicates immediate developments. It is not the final result of the situation but part of its unfolding. Like the recent past, it tends to show conditions that won't last.

7. Self – this card reveals what the person contributes to the situation. It may denote an attitude or an action. You may find this the key card, as I once did in a reading where the Chariot reversed showed that the person lacked the will to carry on with things as they were.

8. Environment – this card shows outside influence on a person. It may refer to someone specific (especially if the reading concerns a relationship), or to the situation in general. In the reading just mentioned, the 3 of Cups reversed in the environment indicated a lack of support from friends.

9. Hopes and fears – this card illuminates what the person expects to happen. Often this position greatly affects the outcome because it shows the subject's attitudes and desires. For instance, the 5 of Swords here would say that he or she feared defeat; and such pessimism can help bring about that defeat. The Star or the 6 of Wands (both cards of confidence) would tend to produce a more positive result. This position sometimes helps the person confront hidden attitudes.

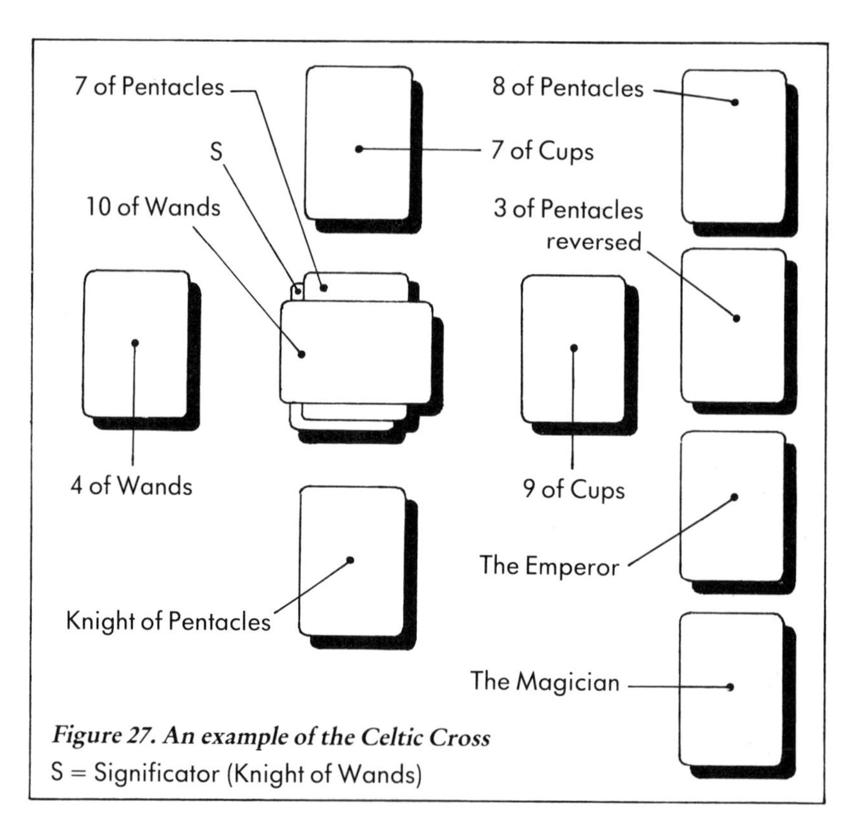

Figure 27. An example of the Celtic Cross
S = Significator (Knight of Wands)

10. Outcome – this card sums up the other nine. Given all the other influences, it shows the way things are likely to turn out.

We should never consider the outcome as fixed. We can always change direction and, in fact, the reading itself, because it shows the way things are going and can, therefore, serve as the starting point for change. At the same time, however, we should not assume that we can alter the outcome without serious effort. The reading shows strong influences on a person's life. Going against those influences can require a good deal of conscious work. If the reading should show some sort of undesirable outcome, it is up to the reader to help the person find ways of improving the situation.

Before leaving the Celtic Cross, we will look at a brief example. The subject has recently finished college and been accepted for medical school. However, he is doubtful about whether he wants to become a doctor. This is his question. For the significator he chooses the Knight of Wands. The cards come out as shown in Figure 27.

1. The first card, the 7 of Pentacles, indicates the value of his achievement so far. His work has led to something very real. Seeing this reality can help him decide what continuing will involve. The card also reveals his pride in what he has done.

2. The 10 of Wands crossing card looks at success from a different point of view. In contrast, it denotes his fear of burdening himself with a career he doesn't really want.

3. The Knight of Pentacles, as the basis, shows the hard work he has done to produce the flowering bush shown in the 7 of Pentacles. As a card of drudgery it represents the drawbacks of that work. The card poses two questions. 'Do I want more of this?' and, 'Can I experience it in some other way?'

4. The 4 of Wands, as recent past, shows his joy at being released from study on leaving college. Again, he has to decide whether he will accept this freedom as a temporary vacation before starting his studies again or as a more important alternative to a medical career.

5. The 7 of Cups, as possible outcome, indicates a potential danger, that none of his plans will come to anything, that he will allow his energy – and the accomplishments of the other 7, the 7 of Pentacles – to melt into daydreams.

6. The 9 of Cups, as the near future, shows him having a good time now that he has left college. By its nature this card depicts a temporary situation.

7. The Magician, in the position of self, emphasizes the subject's power to direct his life and make decisions. But the Magician also acts as a channel for helping others. In one of his many aspects he symbolizes the healing arts. This gives the person a strong indication that becoming a doctor is natural to him, despite his misgivings.

8. The Emperor, in the environment, signifies the pressures of society, and in particular his father, to do the expected thing and continue his education. This card helps him recognize that part of his misgivings comes from the fear of simply following his father's plans for him. If he chooses medical school, he needs to know that he has made the decision himself.

9. The 3 of Pentacles reversed signifies a fear of failure. By demonstrating this fear the card helps him confront it. The person needs to take the same attitude as with the Emperor, recognizing its reality but not allowing it to influence his decision, either for or against. With regard to overcoming the fear, the Magician implies that he can succeed.

10. Finally, the 8 of Pentacles shows a student deeply involved in his studies. The card points strongly to a choice of going on to medical school. The decision, however, remains with him.

The Alphabet Spread: This interesting method, which I have developed, breaks the deck into three separate packs, each with its own character. It allows you to play with such things as your name, the day of the week, other words, and so on.

The alphabet contains twenty-six letters and $26 \times 3 = 78$, the number of cards in the Tarot. Therefore, for this method we first divide the deck into three groups of twenty-six cards. The division in the chart on page 125 is mine but you may wish to create your own.

Because of the Wands' influence the first pack of twenty-six cards will show the active, energetic side of the situation. The second, with Cups, will emphasize the emotional aspects. The third, with Swords, will indicate conflicts. As the practical suit, Pentacles appear in each pack.

You can use the three packs either together or separately. To use them together, choose a word with three letters, for instance, the word NOW. Take the first pack and mix the twenty-six cards. Then, with the first card as A, the second as B, and so on, count down to the letter N. Lay this card on the table. Mix the second pack and count down to the letter O. Mix the third pack and count down to the letter W. You can now read the three selected cards as a picture of the current moment.

Magician	High Priestess	Empress
Emperor	Hierophant	Lovers
Chariot	Strength	Hermit
Wheel of Fortune	Justice	Hanged Man
Death	Temperance	Devil
Tower	Star	Moon
Sun	Judgment	World
Ace of Wands	Ace of Cups	Ace of Swords
2 of Wands	2 of Cups	2 of Swords
3 of Wands	3 of Cups	3 of Swords
4 of Wands	4 of Cups	4 of Swords
5 of Wands	5 of Cups	5 of Swords
6 of Wands	6 of Cups	6 of Swords
7 of Wands	7 of Cups	7 of Swords
8 of Wands	8 of Cups	8 of Swords
9 of Wands	9 of Cups	9 of Swords
10 of Wands	10 of cups	10 of Swords
Page of Wands	Page of Cups	Page of Swords
Knight of Wands	Knight of Cups	Knight of Swords
Queen of Wands	Queen of Cups	Queen of Swords
King of Wands	King of Cups	King of Swords
Ace of Pentacles	4 of Pentacles	8 of Pentacles
2 of Pentacles	5 of Pentacles	9 of Pentacles
3 of Pentacles	6 of Pentacles	10 of Pentacles
Page of Pentacles	7 of Pentacles	Knight of Pentacles
King of Pentacles	Fool	Queen of Pentacles

(You can use the same method, twice, for a six-letter word, such as FUTURE.)

Using the packs separately gives you three different views of the situation, each one emphasizing the quality of that pack. For this method you again choose a word. You might choose TODAY, your name, someone else's name, or a word that refers to a particular situation. Take the first deck and mix it. Counting the first card as A, find all the letters of the word and place them on the table in the proper order to spell the word. (If the word contains a double letter, such as the 'A' in Alan, you can see that card as applying in both positions.) Mix the second

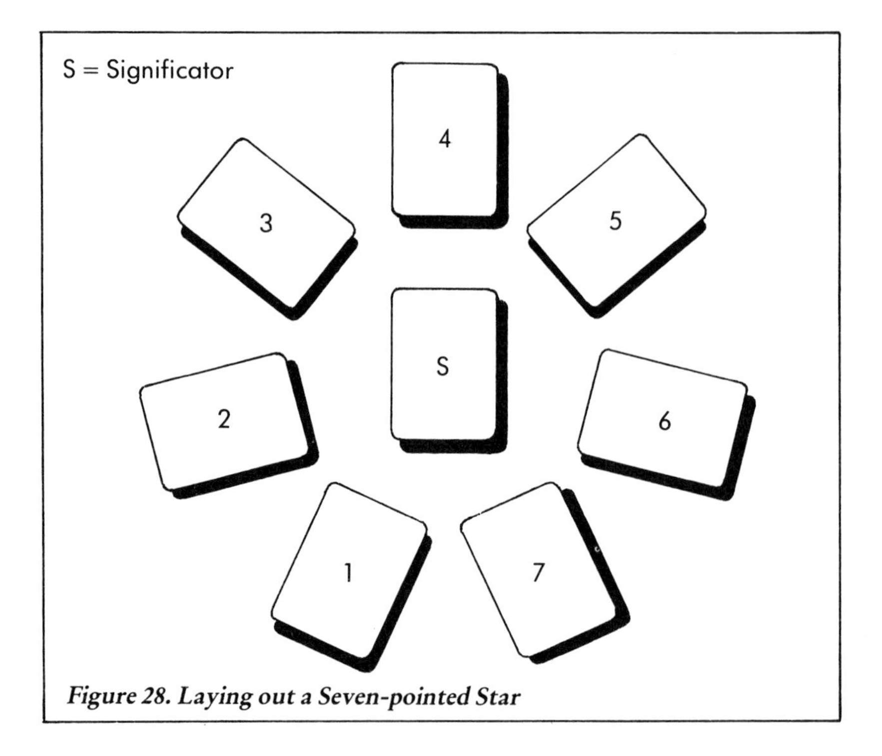

Figure 28. Laying out a Seven-pointed Star

pack and again count out the proper cards, laying them in a row below the first set. Repeat this with the third pack. This method provides three ways of looking at whatever word you have chosen. When you become more experienced you will begin to see connections between the three levels.

The alphabet method works best when you wish to get a general impression from the cards. It helps answer the question, 'How are things going?' either in general, or when applied to a continuing situation.

Calendar Spreads:

1. Seven-Pointed Star (see Figure 28)

This spread allows you to get an overview of the week ahead. With the significator in the middle, turn over seven cards in the pattern.

The first card stands for Sunday, the second for Monday, and so on. (You can, of course, start with whatever day you happen to read the cards.) You can take each image separately, as the

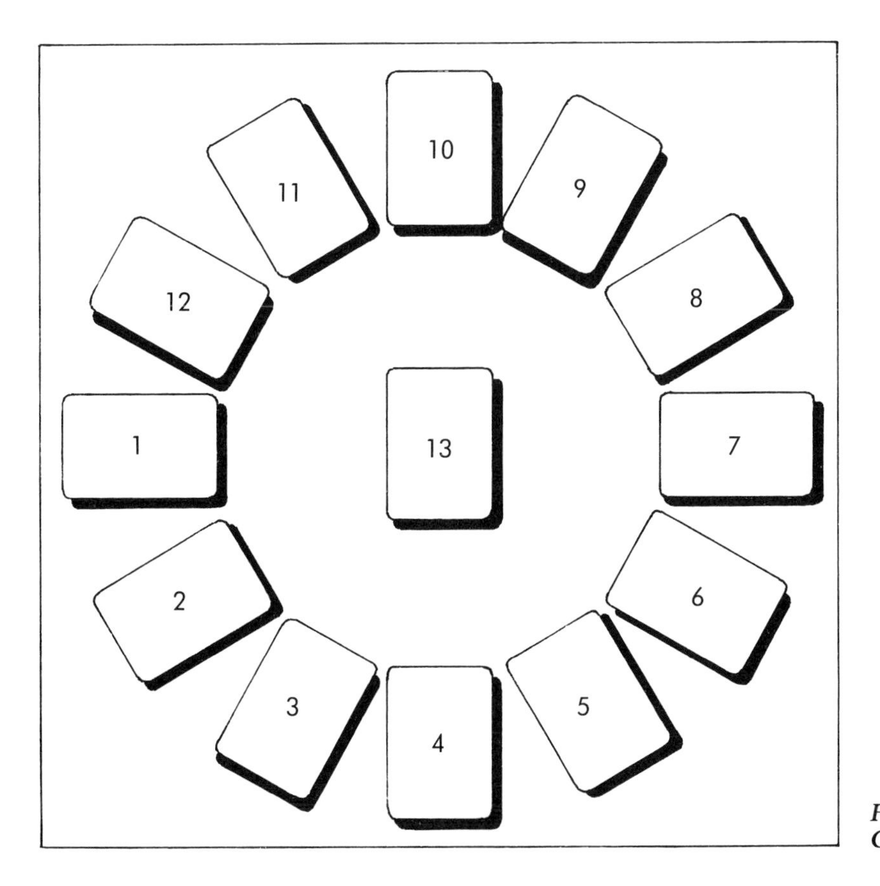

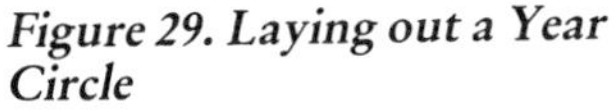
Figure 29. Laying out a Year Circle

characteristic of that day, or see the cards as denoting a progression. For instance, suppose the first two cards are the Fool and Temperance. The Fool describes Sunday as a day to take a chance on something, where you should follow your instincts when faced with a choice. Monday then becomes a day for a more careful look. Having taken the leap, you now need to develop the situation with moderation and planning.

2. Year Circle (see Figure 29)
For this spread a significator is not required. After mixing and cutting the cards, lay them out in the pattern.

The last card, the one in the centre, is actually read first, for it characterizes the year as a whole. For instance, the Chariot in the thirteenth position would tell you that in the year ahead you should take a firm attitude to your life and plans since willpower will bring success. Next, look at each card in turn. Card 1 represents the basic tenor of the coming month, card 2 the month after that, and so on.

In both these readings you might find that one card cannot adequately describe a whole day or a month. You should realize that this kind of reading does not replace the more detailed information that can be derived from, for example; the Celtic Cross. Whatever your year reading says, you can always do other readings to learn about specific situations. Also, as you become experienced with those patterns, you might want to try them with more than one card in each position. This works particularly well with the seven-pointed star, in which two or three cards can give you a more detailed picture for each of the different days.

The Work Cycle (see Figure 30)*:* Most Tarot spreads give information. They also provide images of your life and you can use these to focus your efforts at improvement. Still, primarily they tell you the way things are. The spread illustrated, which I developed, emphasizes what you can do about the situation. Unlike most layouts, it also provides a method for turning over more cards if the first line leaves you without a clear answer to your question.

Choose the significator and mix the cards as usual. Lay the first card on top of the significator and the second across that, as in the Celtic Cross. Then turn over the next seven cards in a

Figure 30. Laying out a Work Cycle

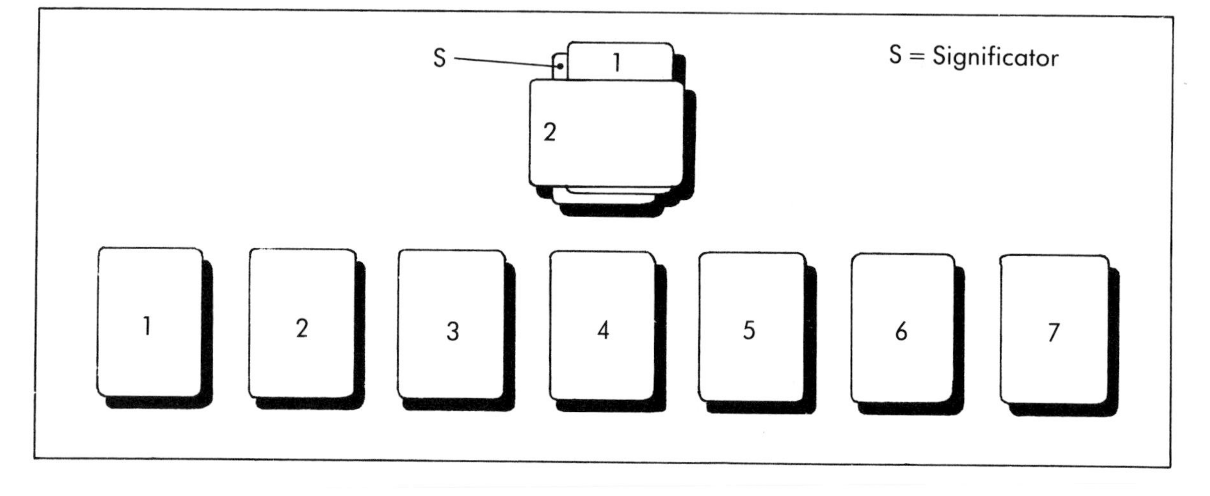

row, placing them below the first two.

Cards 1 and 2 above the row set out the basic situation, similar to the first two cards in the Celtic Cross. Card 1 in the row refers to 'past experience'. It shows part of the background to the situation. Card 2 represents 'expectations'. It indicates the person's attitude, what he or she expects to happen. This helps to identify positive or negative approaches. The next three cards (3, 4, and 5) are read together as the 'work'. They indicate the opportunities and obstacles facing the person.

Card 6 in the row is the 'outcome' and shows the most likely development. Card 7 is the 'result'. It indicates what will happen *because* of the outcome. For instance, suppose that card 6 is the 7 of Cups reversed and card 7 is the King of Pentacles. The 7 of Cups reversed tells a person that he is likely to stop daydreaming and take action on his fantasies. The King of Pentacles assures him that such actions will bring success.

If these cards give you a clear message, then stop there. If you find yourself still seeking understanding, however, you can lay out a second line of seven cards underneath the first row. The same positions will apply. As a group, they will show a different aspect of the situation to the first row, giving the person a chance to look at it from another viewpoint. In principle you can lay out up to ten lines, with five cards left over for a 'commentary'. In practice, I have rarely found the need to go beyond two or three lines. For many readings, the first nine cards will give a firm answer. This spread works best with questions such as, 'What should I do about my problem?' or, 'What is the best way to handle this?' (This could refer to a person, an opportunity, and so on.) You might also ask, 'What approach can I take to get the job?' or, 'How can I deal with my lover?'

The various spreads shown here will give you many possibilities for using the cards to answer your own and other people's questions. As you practise with them, you will begin to find a deeper meaning in the images. Always remember that the cards in no way control people's actions. They merely point the way to understanding those actions as well as their consequences. What you do with your life will, of course, always remain entirely up to you.

RUNES

A runic memorial in Uppland, Sweden. To the Vikings the Runes were endowed with mysterious power and authority and they raised stones such as this one in honour of their warriors and their overseas exploits. The stones are beautifully carved, often with a slender snake, as here.

The Runes, like the Tarot and the *I Ching*, belong to the great systems of divination. Though we use them for fortune telling, they also open the way to an ancient spiritual tradition.

For a long time the Runes were all but forgotten, mentioned only in fantasy novels and horror stories. In recent years, however, many people have found them a particularly valuable method of divination. One reason for this is that anyone can draw them. This means that you can make your own set, on pieces of wood, for example, on ceramics, or on stones. (Instructions are given below.) Doing so creates a personal bond between you and *your* Runes.

The Runes form an ancient Germanic alphabet, once used for normal writing. At the same time, the signs have always carried magical and divinatory meanings. The word 'Rune' derives from the Old Norse 'run' which means 'secret'. The Vikings engraved Runes on the hilts of their swords and built them in the walls of their houses as a protective device to ward off evil. The shamans and healers of Scandinavia used them to heal the sick, to protect burial mounds and to cast spells. Supposedly they used Runes to fly through the air and to call up dead spirits.

They also used them for divination. Wandering rune-masters and rune-mistresses would pass through towns and villages wearing animal skins and blue cloaks (blue was sacred to the god Odin whose connection with Runes is described below). *The Saga of Erik the Red* describes a professional rune-mistress. She wears a cloak set with stones, a hood lined with cat fur, and catskin mittens and shoes. She also carries a staff set with a knob at one end (similar to a magician's wand).

Traditionally the Runes belong to the one-eyed god Odin

('Od' means 'wind' and 'spirit'). Lord of death and rebirth, Odin rode an eight-legged horse and received messages from two ravens. A wolf walked with him on his journeys through the world. To get the Runes Odin hung on the world tree, 'Yggdrasil', for nine days and nights (a link to both the Hanged Man and the Hermit in the Tarot). He also sacrificed his eye to Mimir, guardian of the well of wisdom. To cover his empty eye socket Odin wore a soft-brimmed hat, almost the same hat that is worn by the Magician in some older Tarot decks. (As far as I know, no one has ever investigated the possibility of the Runes as one source for the Tarot.) Many people invoke Odin's aid before casting and reading the Runes. To do so, picture him in your mind and then mentally ask for guidance.

The Runes consist of twenty-four letters together with one blank Rune called 'Wyrd' or 'Fate'. Very briefly, their meanings are as follows:

1. FREY Frey was the god of fertility and peace. This Rune, therefore, means good luck, success, and fertility. It also refers to harmony.

Reversed, it means loss or stagnation and a lack of harmony.

2. POWER This Rune means creative power but also wisdom and knowledge. It stands for good fortune and opportunity but also sexuality.

Reversed, it means opportunities missed, a lack of development, and possible physical problems.

3. THORN (THOR) Thor was the Norse god of strength. This Rune, therefore, means protection. Someone may provide help or good news may come.

Reversed, it can mean bad news or vulnerability. As a thorn it denotes small but not serious dangers.

4. ODIN This Rune represents Odin himself. It signifies wisdom and help from someone older. It can mean magic, psychic power, or initiation.

Reversed, it invokes Odin's trickster side. Someone (and this is especially true of an older person) causes trouble or plays tricks. Beware of advice.

5. WHEEL This Rune can indicate physical journeys, especially pleasant ones, or journeys that bring some positive development. It can also refer to a person's 'spiritual' journey of development.

Reversed, it means a difficult journey or delays. It can also refer to lessons the person must learn.

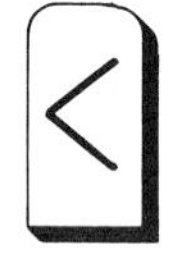

6. FIRE This Rune represents the creative fire – the artistic impulse – but also passion and sexual desire.

Reversed, it means a block or impediment to the person's creative energy.

7. GIFT This is a sign of gifts, generosity, and giving. People come together and relationships become deeper.

Reversed, it means selfishness but also separation. Something may block or harm friendship.

8. JOY A sign of happiness and of harmony between people. A situation may change for the better.

Reversed, it means problems between people, changes that can bring unhappiness. It warns the person to look at situations that might cause trouble.

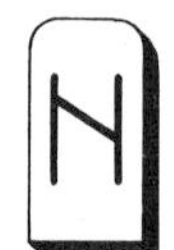

9. HAIL This Rune signifies unexpected setbacks or problems for the person, especially illness.

Reversed, it represents delays, primarily from forces or situations outside the person.

10. NECESSITY This important Rune teaches the lesson of patience. It will not go well if the person tries to push something. Greed or simple desire can prove destructive.

Reversed, it warns the person to avoid quick decisions. He or she should think carefully before making any kind of commitment.

11. ICE This Rune denotes some kind of obstacle. By its imagery it also represents coldness between people.

Reversed, it suggests that this coldness can lead to arguments. However, the person can act positively to try to melt the ice in a more productive way.

12. YEAR This Rune refers to the cycles of nature and of life. Something will come to fruition. Effort receives its reward.

Reversed, it suggests a block in the natural working out of things. Removed, matters will reach their proper conclusion.

13. YEW The yew tree was sacred to Odin who gathered the dead souls for their journey to Valhalla or the Underworld. This Rune, therefore, signifies the solemn importance of death in human life. We can interpret it like Death in the Tarot (the thirteenth trump) as denoting the passing of old ways and habits.

Reversed, it means that the person hangs on to old patterns. It can also represent an emotional difficulty with regard to death.

14. HEARTH By its symbolism this Rune refers to the home. Traditionally it signifies mystery. Things may not be what they seem. The person may need to look below the surface.

Reversed, it means that secrets are revealed and feelings openly expressed.

15. PROTECTION This Rune signifies protection from danger. The person may face a temptation but will resist it. New beginnings are possible.

Reversed, it indicates some danger which the person needs to avoid. This may come from someone else.

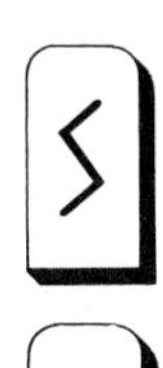

16. THE SUN A Rune of good health and happiness, it also denotes the creative will. It can signify guidance.

Reversed, it indicates the danger of illness from carelessness.

17. TYR Tyr was the god of war. This Rune signifies courage and energy but also passion bringing happiness.

Reversed, it indicates that conflicts drain the person. It is a mark of frustration.

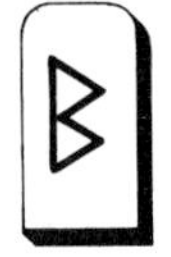

18. BIRTH This Rune can refer to an actual birth or new marriage but also to beginnings and growth, the start of something significant.

Reversed, it indicates stagnation or obstacles that prevent the birth of something.

19. HORSE This Rune signifies travel but also change, such as a new job or a new home. It can refer to spiritual journeys.

Reversed, it indicates restlessness. The person wishes to travel as an escape.

20. MAN The image of a human being suggests intelligence, memory, and culture, all the attributes that set humans apart. The Rune also refers to family matters.

Reversed, it indicates that the person seeks isolation, especially from family. It can also mean not using intelligence.

21. WATER Water symbolizes the unconscious, intuition, and mystery. This Rune indicates psychic awareness but also the hidden sources of creativity.

Reversed, it means that the water has become stormy. The person becomes emotional but confused.

22. FERTILITY This Rune indicates completion, whether of projects or ideas or in the sense of people developing to their fullest potential.

Reversed, it shows a block to that development. The person needs to work harder.

23. DAY This is a Rune of awakening and clarity. It indicates success, wealth, and abundance in life.

Reversed, it means that the person needs to be careful and to conserve resources.

24. ANCESTRAL PROPERTY This Rune refers to inheritances and to property in general. It can also describe inherited abilities or family traditions.

Reversed, it signifies that there are problems with inheritance, difficulties with parents, or a break with family.

25. WYRD (FATE) The rune-master's bag contains a blank Rune, signifying mystery but also fate. In a reading it indicates something the person cannot know. It also tells him or her that fate may decide the issue.

You can draw your Runes on paper or cardboard and will be

able to use them in this form for divination. You may, however, wish to follow tradition and make a set out of wood. If possible, use yew, ash, or oak, all of which are sacred trees. Cut twenty-five pieces, each about 5cm (2in) high and 2cm (¾in) wide. Round the edges, rounding one side somewhat more to represent the top. You can then carve the Runes or paint them on the wood. The ancient rune-masters used their own blood; most people today prefer to use red or blue paint! Remember to leave one Rune blank for Wyrd. As an alternative to wood, collect twenty-five pebbles or small stones, all about the same size and with at least one flat side on which to paint the Runes.

Most people keep their Runes in a leather or suede pouch, which is useful for casting as well as storage. To cast the Runes, mix them in their pouch and then empty them on to a flat surface, such as a table top or a cloth spread out on the floor. Only interpret those which fall face up (see Figure 31). If you find that there are too many of these, return the face-up Runes to the bag and mix and cast them again, reading the face-up ones from this smaller group. If Runes fall together, try to see how their meanings combine or affect each other.

If you prefer to use 'spreads', as with the Tarot, mix the Runes in their pouch, then draw out the correct number, laying them down in their proper positions. Most of the Tarot layouts will work just as well with the Runes. One special one is the Cross of Thor which uses five Runes in the following positions:

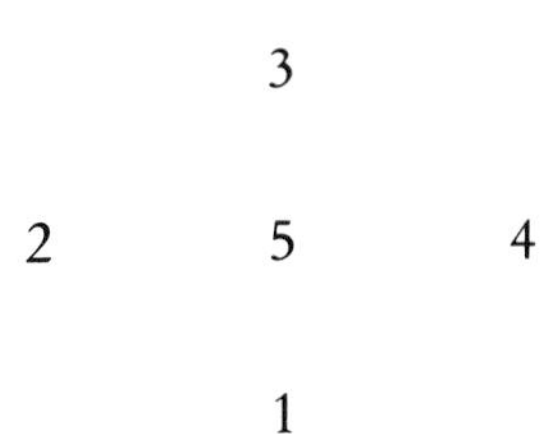

Here 1 represents the general situation, 2 obstacles, 3 helpful influences, 4 the immediate outcome, and 5 the long-term results.

Figure 31. Casting a set of wooden Runes

SOME METHODS OF DIVINATION

As mentioned in the Introduction people have used virtually everything to tell fortunes. In ancient Greece people practised phyllordomancy – beating the hand with rose petals and taking omens by the sound. People have examined onions (cromniomancy) to find the name of a future spouse. There is even a system – geloscopy – involving signs determined by laughter.

If some of these methods seem exotic to us, others are more practical, if simplistic. For instance, lampadomancy consists of signs read from the flame of a burning torch or oil lamp. One or three points of flame indicate good luck. Two points show bad luck. A bent flame denotes the danger of sickness. If the flame suddenly snuffs out it suggests potential disaster.

Foretelling the future by sand pictures. This method of reading the images in the sand has been practised by Arab 'wise men' for centuries.

SORTILEGE

A more interesting and complex system is sortilege. This consists of drawing lots to determine a reading. Related to Runes, it was also practised in Germany from medieval times on, as well as in many other places. There are many methods of sortilege. Aleuromancy is one. It consists of writing possible answers or developments on scraps of paper, then rolling these up in pieces of dough and baking them. One is then chosen and broken open to find the answer. The fortune cookies served in many Chinese restaurants are a form of aleuromancy.

The easiest method of sortilege is to place slips of paper in a box and draw one. For more elaborate systems people have used arrows, the ankle bones of sheep, carved bones, shells, stones, and coloured sticks. In most of these cases the diviner or the subject casts the pieces on to the ground or a surface and the

The Japanese believe strongly in fortune telling and many people still consult the 'uranaisha' or fortune teller regularly. The photograph shows the fortune teller of the Inari, or Fox Temple, at Kyoto being consulted to see whether the omens are good or not.

diviner then reads them in a manner similar to reading the Runes. In some African systems the diviner doesn't so much read the individual pieces as the overall picture they form, a little like a highly sophisticated version of reading the pictures formed by tea leaves. An interesting aspect of African divination is that instead of the simple formulae we have with, for example, tea leaves (such as good luck, bad luck, health, illness, and so on) the meanings often involve ritualized poetry.

One overall feature of sortilege is the opportunity to create your own system. As with the Runes you can do this on paper or cards but you will probably want to use wood or stones. Choose a set of symbols. For instance, you might choose the sun for happiness and simplicity, knives for conflict, a lunar crescent for mystery or imagination, a flower for love, and so on. Working with other systems, such as the Tarot or tea leaves, will give you a sense of which symbols speak to you in a powerful way. If you practise crystal ball gazing or some other form of scrying you will discover natural symbols from your own unconscious. Do not use too many. Nine, as a lunar number, works well for many people. When you have worked out your symbols, paint them on the wood or stones. If you use stones, choose round ones with fairly flat sides.

When you wish to use your oracle, hold the stones or lots in your hand, shake them and then cast them on to the reading surface. Remove those which have fallen face down. Those remaining form the reading. The ones nearest you indicate influences closer in time or space. Signs that fall near each other can be read in combination. As with tea leaves look for the overall message formed by the images.

CLEROMANCY – DIVINATION BY DICE

Dice have existed for thousands of years and, while people have used them for gambling and in games, they possibly originated as a method of fortune telling. There are many kinds of dice besides the common ones in use in Western countries. The Romans used 'astragals' or sheep bones.

To divine with dice, use three rather than two. Draw a circle 30.5cm (12in) in diameter. Mix the dice in a cup or your hand and cast them into the circle. If all three fall outside try again. If this happens a second time abandon the reading and try again the following day.

The basic reading consists of adding the numbers and consulting the list given below. If one dice falls outside the oracle it indicates a block to the developments shown in the reading. If two dice fall outside the circle they warn of possible quarrels. However, if one or more fall outside and the number within adds up to less than three, the dice have nothing to say.

A sixteenth-century engraving showing young girls throwing dice to foretell how long they would live.

3. Unexpected but favourable developments
4. Disappointment or discontent
5. Something you want will come to you but possibly in an unexpected way; you might receive good news

6. Discouragement, especially in business
7. Delays, possibly trouble through gossip
8. Strong influences from outside
9. An omen of love and harmony; if after a quarrel, reconciliation
10. Birth, promotions, new beginnings
11. Parting with a loved one
12. A letter bringing good news
13. An unhappy development
14. A friend helps you or a new acquaintance becomes a friend
15. Be careful; avoid temptation
16. A good sign for travel
17. A change of plans
18. Happiness, success

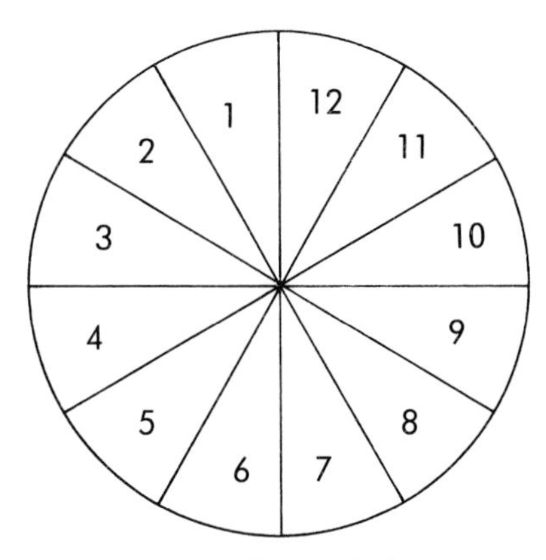

Figure 32. Dividing a circle for cleromancy

For a more complex reading, divide the circle into twelve sections (see Figure 32). If a die falls into a section it refers to that subject. The divisions of the circle are as follows:

1. Coming year
2. Money questions
3. Travel
4. Home
5. Present concerns
6. Health
7. Love and relationships
8. Legal issues
9. Current state of mind
10. Work, career
11. Friends
12. Enemies

The omens for the numbers on the individual dice are as follows:

1. Favourable, but requiring caution
2. Need for good relations with others
3. Success
4. Disappointment
5. Good developments
6. Uncertainty

While this method gives a slightly more complex reading, divination by dice remains rather rigid, leaving little room for intuition or interpretation.

CARTOMANCY

Ordinary playing cards can serve for divination as well as Tarot cards. In comparison with the Tarot's pictures and symbolism, however, the meanings are much more simplistic.

A Parisian fortune teller of the 1790s. During the uncertain times of the French Revolution people flocked to have their fortunes told and one of the most popular methods was using card layouts. However, ordinary playing cards as shown in the illustration do not offer the complexity of Tarot card readings and usually covered subjects such as love and marriage, and dark strangers!

Hearts:
Ace – happiness, love, friendship
King – a fair-haired man, affectionate and generous but impetuous
Queen – a fair-haired woman, trustworthy
Jack – a fair-haired young person; a good friend
10 Good fortune, happiness
9 The 'wish card'; desires come true
8 Invitations, but also partings
7 Someone is unreliable
6 Unexpected good fortune; generosity
5 Jealousy, indecision
4 Changes, possibly travel or postponements
3 Need for caution
2 Success, friendship

Spades:
Ace – conflicts, a difficult love affair
King – dark-haired man, ambitious, usually successful
Queen – dark-haired woman, can be seductive or unscrupulous

Jack – dark-haired young man; a well-meaning person
10 Worry
9 Bad luck, can mean delays or quarrels
8 Disappointments and opposition
7 A warning against possible loss of friendship
6 An improvement in the person's life
5 Anxiety, setbacks, interferences
4 Jealousy, business troubles
3 Partings, possibly due to faithlessness
2 Scandal, gossip, danger of deceit

Diamonds:
Ace – money, a ring
King – fair-haired man, stubborn and powerful
Queen – fair-haired woman, flirtatious, sophisticated, witty
Jack – a relative, someone not quite reliable
10 Journey, changes, usually bringing wealth
9 Opportunities and surprises, usually financial
8 Late marriage or a new relationship; unexpected money
7 A gift
6 A reconciliation; a warning against a possible second marriage
5 Successful meetings, particularly in business
4 An inheritance, a change for the better
3 Legal or domestic battles
2 A love affair becomes more important than hitherto.

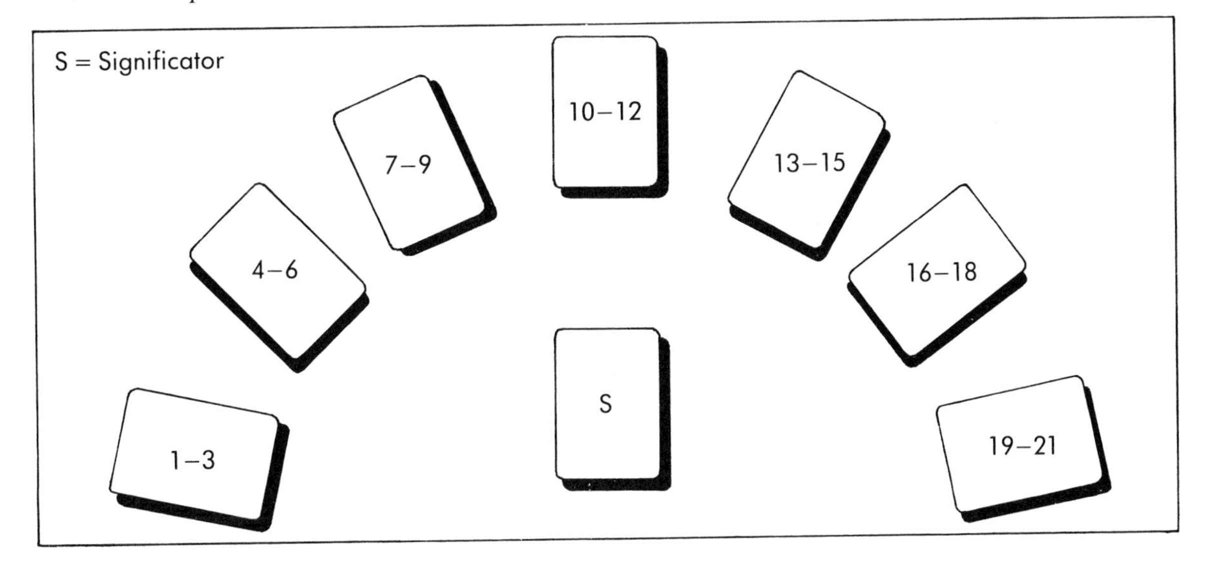

Figure 33. A traditional card layout

Clubs:

Ace – harmony, property, achievements, love
King – dark-haired man, honest, open
Queen – dark-haired woman, strong-minded, helpful, attractive
Jack – a reliable friend
10 Money from an unexpected source, good luck or a gift
9 A new romance
8 Opposition, danger of recklessness
7 Prosperity, though a danger of romantic interference
6 Business success
5 Help from a friend or spouse
4 Bad change of fortune
3 Good marriage or alliance
2 Disappointment and opposition

To read the cards you can use most of the spreads described with the Tarot. One difference: mix the cards yourself and then open them in a fan and ask the person to choose the correct number of cards for the layout.

If the spread calls for a significator follow the table below:

fair or grey-haired man over 40 – King of Diamonds
fair or grey-haired woman over 40 – Queen of Diamonds
fair-haired young man – King of Hearts
fair-haired young woman – Queen of Hearts
dark-haired man over 40 – King of Spades
dark-haired woman over 40 – Queen of Spades
dark-haired young man – King of Clubs
dark-haired young woman – Queen of Clubs

For a traditional layout ask the subject to divide the deck into two halves and then choose one. Lay down the top twenty-one cards in seven groups of three in a semicircle around the significator (see Figure 33). Cards 1–3 represent the situation and the person's state of mind; 4–6 signify family or relationships; 7–9 show present desires; 10-12 show long-term expectations; 13–15 indicate the unexpected; 16-18 signify the immediate developments; 19–21 the long-term results.

FURTHER READING

INTRODUCTION

Baynes, C.F. and Wilhelm, R. (translators) *I Ching or Book of Changes* (translated from Chinese and German), (Princeton University Press, 1967; Routledge Kegan Paul, 1983)

PALMISTRY

Benham, W.G. *The Laws of Scientific Hand Reading* (Duell, Sloan and Pierce, 1946)

'Cheiro' *Book of Fate and Fortune* (Arrow Books, 1985)

Guide to the Hand (Barrie & Jenkins, 1913)

Gettings, Fred *Palmistry Made Easy* (Wilshire Book Company, 1967)

Hipskind, Judith *Palmistry – the Whole View* (Llewellyn Publications, 1983)

Luxon, Bettina and Goolden, Jill *Your Hand: Simple Palmistry for Everyone* (Heinemann, 1983; Crown Publishers Inc, 1984)

Newcomer-Bramblett, Esther *Reading Hands for Pleasure or Profit* (Woods Publications, 1982)

CRYSTAL BALL GAZING

Ferguson, Sibyl *The Crystal Ball* (Samuel Weiser Inc, 1980)

Melville, John *Crystal Gazing and Clairvoyance* (Samuel Weiser Inc, 1970; Aquarian Press Ltd, 1979)

THE TAROT

Case, Paul Foster *The Tarot: A Key to the Wisdom of the Ages* (Macoy Publishing Co, Virginia, 1977)

Cavendish, Richard *The Tarot* (Michael Joseph, 1975)

Crowley, Aleister *The Book of Thoth* (Samuel Weiser Inc, 1974). First published 1944

Gray, E. *Complete Guide to the Tarot* (Bantam, 1971)

Kaplan, Stuart *The Encyclopedia of Tarot Vol. I and II* (U.S. Games Syst, 1978 (Vol. I) and 1985 (Vol. II); Vol. I, Aquarian Press Ltd, 1979)

Peach, Emily *Tarot Workbook: Understanding and Using Tarot Symbolism* (Aquarian Press Ltd, 1984)

Pollack, Rachel *Tarot: The Open Labyrinth* (Aquarian Press Ltd, 1986)

Salvador Dali's Tarot (Salem House, 1985; Michael Joseph, 1985)

Seventy Eight Degrees of Wisdom: Book of Tarot, Part I – The Major Arcana; Part 2 – The Minor Arcana and Readings (Aquarian Press Ltd, 1980, Part 1; 1983, Part 2)

Waite, A.E. *The Pictorial Key to the Tarot* (Rider, London, 1971). First published 1910

Walker, Barbara G. *Secrets of the Tarot, Origins, History and Symbolism* (Harper and Row, 1985)

RUNES

Howard, Michael A. *The Magic of the Runes* (Samuel Weiser Inc, 1980; Aquarian Press Ltd, 1980)

Thorsson, Edred *Futhark: A Handbook of Rune Magic* (Samuel Weiser Inc, 1984)

Willis, Tony *Runic Workbook: Understanding and Using the Power of Runes* (Aquarian Press Ltd, 1986)

ILLUSTRATION ACKNOWLEDGMENTS

BBC Hulton Picture Library: Pages 19, 51, 57 and 137.
Mary Evans Picture Library: Pages 5, 8, 9, 66 (Harry Price Collection, University of London) and 68.
The Mansell Collection: Pages 58, 62 and 69.
The Rainbird Publishing Group Limited: Pages 60 (British Museum, *The Magus* by Francis Barrett, London 1801, fig. 79), 65 both (Bibliothèque Nationale, Pariş), 67 (Sylvia Mann Collection) and 70 both (The Portal Gallery, EON Productions).
Rider & Company, London: Pages 75, 79, 83, 89, 96, 103 and 108.
Roger-Viollet, Paris: Pages 16, 136, 138 and 140.
Topham Picture Library: Pages 48 and 130.

INDEX

Page numbers in *italic* refer to illustrations